SAN FRANCISCO'S
49-MILE
SCENIC DRIVE

THE GUIDEBOOK

Joseph M. Lubow
Laurel Rosen

SASQUATCH
BOOKS
SEATTLE

Printed in the United States of America
Distributed in Canada by Raincoast Books, Ltd.

First edition
07 06 05 04 03 02 01   5 4 3 2 1

Cover Illustration: Neal Aspinall
Cover & Interior Design: Kate Basart
Maps: GreenEye Design

We used many sources in our research. Of particular importance are the following: *Walking San Francisco on the Barbary Coast Trail*, by Daniel Bacon (Quicksilver Press, 1997), *San Francisco: The Ultimate Guide*, by Randolph Delehanty (Chronicle Books, 1995), *San Francisco*, by Tom Downs (Lonely Planet Publications, 2nd ed. 1999), *San Francisco Almanac*, by Gladys Hansen (Chronicle Books, 1995).

Permission for use of the 49-Mile Scenic Drive seagull sign granted by the Department of Parking and Traffic and the San Francisco Convention and Visitors Bureau.

Permission for use of the artwork from the original 1954 map of the 49-Mile Scenic Drive granted by the Downtown Association of San Francisco.

Library of Congress Cataloging-in-Publication Data
Lubow, Joseph M.
    San Francisco's 49-mile scenic drive : the guidebook / by Joseph Lubow and Laurel Rosen.
        p.   cm.
ISBN 1-57061-251-X
    1. San Francisco Bay Area (Calif.) — Tours. 2. San Francisco Bay Area (Calif.) — History, Local. 3. Scenic byways — California — San Francisco Bay Area — Guidebooks. 4. Automobile travel — California — San Francisco Bay Area — Guidebooks. I. Rosen, Laurel. II. Title.

F869.S33 L83 2001
979.4'6 — dc21   00-052266

Sasquatch Books
615 Second Avenue
Seattle, Washington 98104
206/467-4300
books@SasquatchBooks.com
www.SasquatchBooks.com

CONTENTS

ACKNOWLEDGMENTS

THE AUTHORS THANK / This project was conceived by Betsy Nolan of the Betsy Nolan Literary Agency and was realized because of her vision and determination—our sincerest thanks to her. Thanks to Jennie McDonald, our inspirational editor, for helping to make this a better book; to Laura Gronewold, our cheerful production editor; and to Kate Basart, who created the wonderful design you see.

Thanks to Carolyn Dee of the Downtown Association of San Francisco, Jim Mathias at the San Francisco Chamber of Commerce, Laurie Armstrong at the San Francisco Convention and Visitors Bureau, and Bond Yee and Amanuel Haile at the San Francisco Department of Parking and Traffic. The San Francisco and Santa Cruz Public Libraries and the *San Francisco Chronicle* provided a wealth of information. Articles by Carl Nolte and Glen Martin were particularly enlightening.

Many friends helped test drive our directions and read early drafts of the book: Kate McLean, Lou Jones, Marisa Meltzer, Jeremy Campbell, Jesse Zeifman, Diane Chin, and Don Hesse.

LAUREL ROSEN THANKS / Leah Garchik is a friend and mentor of the highest order. I thank her for inspiring me in the craft of writing and love of San Francisco. Thanks to Scott Ostler, who taught me to find stories in the everyday scenery of city streets. For their constant support and never-ending love, I thank my dear friends Rebekah Krell and Sanjai Moses, and my family, Marcia, Al, and Rebecca Rosen.

I thank Joe Lubow for inviting me to share in the writing of this book and for sharing his experience and insights with me. I also thank Joe's 1986 Toyota for transporting us on countless rounds of the Drive.

JOSEPH LUBOW THANKS / Laurel Rosen brought a fresh eye to this book. I thank her for her strong writing and researching, and for being a great co-author in every way.

I also thank David Steinberg, Helen Behar, Maggie Paul, Susan Drake, Don Monkerud, Steve Turner, Bill Friedland, Michael Wreszin, and, especially, Shauna Gunderson. Thanks to my sister, Marsha Lubow, who gave me her support and love during this 18-month process.

To Bill Belton and Edmund Jean Louis Brindamour, my recently deceased mentors in life: I think of you always.

INTRODUCTION

WELCOME TO SAN FRANCISCO

San Franciscans say they could travel anywhere in the world and be hard pressed to find a place as beautiful as their very own home. And that's not just provincial pride. Even visitors find the city spectacular—as much for its natural environment as for its human-made scene. Seen from the air, San Francisco Bay looks almost peaceful, with high hills protecting its waters from the rough winds that kick up the ocean just to the west. The drive into town reveals that this pastel-colored city has more than its physical setting to impress visitors. Add the abundance of arts, food, entertainment, and shopping to the superb setting of our hills, ocean, and bay, and it's a wonder that everybody who visits doesn't move to San Francisco.

There's something here for everyone: the bustle of the Financial District, a tranquil walk along Ocean Beach, the sweet and sour tastes of Chinatown, the astonishing views from atop our proud peaks, a Giants' home run splashing into the Bay, a scream of delight from kids playing in Golden Gate Park, or an evening stroll through the French Quarter. Some visitors flock together like seagulls at famous tourist spots such as Fisherman's Wharf; others get cozy in a neighborhood coffeehouse, fly a kite on the Marina Green, or grab a burrito lunch in the Mission District.

San Francisco's deepest essence may indeed be found in the feeling on its streets. Naturally, visitors want to see the whole city. But the top of Twin Peaks, which offers one of the greatest views in urban America, is a good distance from North Beach, and the famous cable cars cover only a fraction of the city's area. What looks on a map like one big city is in reality a network of charming villages, each with its own history and its own distinctive flavor.

Navigating San Francisco is difficult. Its one-way streets, steep hills, and lack of downtown parking are all daunting. Strange quirks permeate the city plan: numbered streets never meet numbered avenues, and thoroughfares that look fine on the map traverse hills that turn them into roller-coaster rides. Pronouncing some of our street names—Gough, for example—can be a challenge too. ("Gow"?

"Go"? Nope—it's "Guff.") But
with good direction, a drive
through San Francisco can
offer the most efficient and scenic way to see and enjoy our spectacular city.

Far and away the best tool for exploring the
whole city is an often-overlooked gem called the 49-Mile Scenic
Drive. Surprisingly, some guidebooks mention it only parentheti-
cally, and most ignore it completely. Yet the Drive not only highlights many of the city's major sights and breathtaking vistas but
dives into its fascinating neighborhoods as well.

HISTORY OF THE 49-MILE SCENIC DRIVE

The 49-Mile Scenic Drive opened with great fanfare on
September 14, 1938, when famed flier Douglas "Wrong Way"
Corrigan—who two months earlier had gained notoriety by
"mistakenly" ending up in Dublin after taking off from New York
and claiming to be headed for Los Angeles—drove it backwards.
(The accounts don't seem to say whether he drove the entire way in
reverse or whether he traversed the route from finish to start, but we
don't recommend that you give either a try, particularly now that the
Drive includes so many one-way streets.)

The Drive was the brainchild of the Downtown Association. The
route was designed to highlight the region's natural beauty and
potential for commerce while promoting San Francisco as a tourist
and business destination. The timing of the Drive's inauguration was
no coincidence—it was a sideshow attraction for the soon-to-be-
opened Golden Gate International Exposition of 1939–40. Just a
few months before the Drive's official opening, in fact, President
Roosevelt had taken a tour of it during a visit to San Francisco.

The 1938 version of the Drive started at City Hall and ended at
Treasure Island, site of the upcoming world's fair. This original route,
according to the *San Francisco News*, was called the "50-Mile Scenic
Drive." By the time the next article on the proposal appeared in the
News, an identical map was marked "49-Mile Scenic Drive." Maybe

the streets shrank or maybe somebody's odometer was on the blink, but more likely the switch to 49 miles was the work of a marketing mind. With San Francisco's area comprising approximately 49 square miles, and the city's famed Gold Rush having taken place in 1849, the new figure was too good to pass up.

Until 1955, the city used blue-and-gold triangular signs to mark the 49-Mile Scenic Drive. In that year, the Downtown Association held a contest to find a new sign to designate the route. The winner—and still the champion today—was a blue-and-white seagull sign with orange text, designed by local artist Rex May.

With the closing of the Golden Gate International Exhibition in 1940 and the transfer of Treasure Island to the Navy, the Drive underwent its first of many reroutings. During World War II, it was temporarily closed because of tightened security in the Presidio and along the waterfronts. When it reopened in 1947, the Drive had been expanded to include more of the eastern half of the city. As highways have been developed and neighborhoods have changed, the Drive—much like the city it celebrates—has been altered over time The last major change prior to the publication of this book was in 1999. In 2000-2001 the Department of Traffic and Parking checked the route's sign placement for accuracy and agreed to begin to correct the signage. Work is progressing, but in the meantime, when there's a discrepancy between the signs and the book, we urge you to follow our directions.

THE DRIVE

San Francisco is the only U.S. city to have set out a marked driving route that allows visitors and residents alike to see and feel most of the city's sights and many of its neighborhoods. The unique 49-Mile Scenic Drive not only takes us to San Francisco's major museums and spectacles, it explores the culture of everyday life in the small villagelike communities within the city limits.

The 49-Mile Scenic Drive starts at City Hall, on the western end of Civic Center Plaza. It travels up to Cathedral Hill and down to Japantown, then heads downtown to the shopping district of Union Square. Following cable car tracks for a bit, the route ventures up still-fashionable Nob Hill, down into Chinatown, through the once-Italian, then-Beatnik stomping grounds of North Beach, and out to tourist-thronged Fisherman's Wharf. Continuing around the bay's shore past Fort Mason, it leads the visitor into the parking lot of the locals' "playground" at the Marina Green.

The Drive then passes the Palace of Fine Arts—the only building left from the Panama-Pacific International Exposition, now housing the Exploratorium, a premier hands-on science museum—and heads into the Marina District. From there, it meanders through the Presidio, a National Park with gorgeous views of the Golden Gate Bridge and the Marin Headlands, and into the prestigious beachside Sea Cliff neighborhood.

The route cuts through Lincoln Park, passing the fine-arts museum at the Palace of the Legion of Honor. It heads west to the historic Cliff House, then turns south, traveling along Ocean Beach, past the Zoo, and around Lake Merced. Passing San Francisco State University, the Drive takes a fairly straight shot north through the residential Sunset District before winding through the city's famous Golden Gate Park. Then, skirting the legendary Haight-Ashbury, it runs through the campus of the University of California, San Francisco, circles eucalyptus-covered Mount Sutro, and snakes up to the summit of Twin Peaks, where the splendor of San Francisco is spread below.

Next, the seagull signs direct the visitor down to the Eureka Valley floor and along the edge of the Castro District. Turning south on Dolores Street, the Drive traces the boundary between the Mission District and Noe Valley. Running east on Cesar Chavez Street, it joins Interstate 280 North, passes over the houseboats in China Basin, and then exits the freeway at the San Francisco Giants' Pacific Bell Park.

Following the border of "Multimedia Gulch," the route travels along the Embarcadero to the Ferry Building. From there the Drive winds through the skyscraper-lined streets of the Financial District, heads west through the South of Market (SoMa) district on Howard Street, and ends where it began, at City Hall.

HOW TO USE THIS BOOK

We didn't set out to write just another guidebook to San Francisco. Rather than focusing exclusively on *what* to see, this book shows you, in a unique way, *how* to explore the city. The route is generally easy to follow by car. (And for those who prefer not to drive, we've provided bus and walking directions at the end of each segment.)

You can use this book in several ways. For an overview, drive the Drive as an entire loop, seeing the city from the car without stopping to investigate the sights. Done in this way, the 49-Mile Scenic Drive will take about three-and-a-half to four hours to navigate. If that feels like too much driving, break the route into two half-day trips. Or tackle one piece of the Drive at a time, spending several days exploring all there is to see along it. For the most rewarding visit, drive the whole 49-Mile Scenic Drive, and then go back another day or on succeeding days to those segments or sights you want to explore in detail.

We have organized this book by dividing the Drive into fourteen segments. Each segment gives specifics on how to get from one place to another, traffic and parking expectations, and interesting detours you might like to take. The segment can easily represent a half-day or a full-day trip, though the length of time it will take you to do each will depend upon how thoroughly you want to see a specific area.

You'll notice that the segments are of unequal length: they range from just under one mile to almost ten, each reflecting the route's simplicity or complexity. Civic Center, which includes City Hall's fine museum, the new San Francisco Library, Civic Center Plaza, and the future home of the Asian Art Museum, offers a lot of things to see in a very small area. In contrast, the western waterfront segment, which includes Ocean Beach, Lake Merced, and the Outer Sunset District, covers lots of scenic territory but contains fewer formal "sights" to stop and behold.

San Francisco is rich with treasures. Many of these are located directly on the 49-Mile Scenic Drive; these sights are noted with a seagull at the beginning of each segment and are numbered in blue throughout the text. Of course, the Drive doesn't touch every sight, so in order to introduce you to the ones near the Drive but not directly on it, we have interwoven off-the-drive sights (marked with gray numbers) into each segment, placing them where detours are most convenient.

The beauty of the 49-Mile Scenic Drive is that the route is marked with those easy-to-see blue-and-white seagull signs and directional arrows. We have done our best to coordinate this book with the city signs and with the Convention and Visitors Bureau maps, but as you use it you may encounter some discrepancies—traffic patterns are unpredictable and will change over time. And while the seagull signs are helpful, remember that we have written our directions in such a way that you can follow the 49-Mile Scenic Drive without them. No matter what surprises you may encounter along the Drive, rest assured that if you follow our directions, you will be successful in navigating your way through one of the most incredible cities on earth.

WHAT YOU NEED TO KNOW

Run by the San Francisco Convention and Visitors Bureau, the **San Francisco Visitor Information Center** is on an outdoor sub-mezzanine level at Hallidie Plaza (Fifth and Market Streets). The VIC offers information, maps, hotel reservations, and other traveler's aids; materials are available in several languages. (It also provides, for a fee, access to your e-mail—a handy attraction for both business and recreational visitors to San Francisco.) The center is open Monday through Friday 9am to 5pm, Saturday and Sunday 9am to 3pm.

DRIVING

Driving in San Francisco requires a certain amount of precaution and a whole lot of savvy. Here are a few tips to ensure that your 49-Mile Scenic Drive doesn't become a 49-Mile Hellish Drive.

Drivers share the road with many other forms of transit. Remember that pedestrians, bicyclists, and cable cars *always* have the right of way. Buses do not necessarily have the right of way, but be prepared for them to take it anyway.

The "Don't block the box" rule you learned in driving school applies more in San Francisco than almost anywhere else because of the narrow streets and steep hills. Help prevent gridlock by making sure you enter an intersection only when you can definitely get all the way through it.

Red-light running has become a real problem on San Francisco streets. To discourage drivers from this dangerous practice, the city has installed a number of red-light cameras which capture on film the license plate number of each vehicle that blows through a red light and the face of its driver. In short order, the offender receives a ticket in the mail—carrying a minimum fine of $271.

The times to be off the streets entirely—especially in the downtown area—with your car securely parked in a legal spot are between 6am and 9am weekday mornings and between 4pm and 7pm weekday afternoons. (Lunchtime can be pretty awful too.)

Most streets in San Francisco are residential, so they generally carry a speed limit of 25 miles per hour and tend to be studded with four-way stops. However, there are a few quick thoroughfares with timed lights designed for carrying high-volume traffic. When navigating from one end of the city to another, try using Oak/Fell and Bush/Pine for east/west traffic from and to downtown; for north/south travel west of Van Ness Avenue, try Franklin/Gough. Other major boulevards without timed lights are also good to know about; these include Geary, Columbus Avenue, Lincoln Boulevard, Van Ness Avenue, 19th Avenue, Sunset Boulevard, Lombard Street, Mission Street, Upper Market Street, Portola Drive, Sloat Avenue, King Street, the Embarcadero, Bay Street, and Marina Boulevard.

Please be careful when turning across train and cable tracks. And keep an eye out for bicyclists; there are no bike lanes downtown, where traffic is heaviest, and streets are often narrow.

When you come to a stop on a steep uphill street, be sure to leave a few feet between your car and the one in front of you. Standard-transmission cars will generally slip back a couple of feet when starting up, and you don't want to be the unlucky car behind them!

PARKING

Be forewarned: Parking in San Francisco is very difficult. We have provided specific parking tips at the end of each segment of the Drive, but here are a few bits of general advice to keep in mind.

Like laundry machines, parking meters in San Francisco accept *only* quarters. Meters are in effect Monday through Saturday from 8am to 6pm. Do yourself a favor and stash a stock of quarters in your glove box before you head out.

It sounds obvious, but we're going to say it anyway: When you park on the street, be sure to read the signs and the parking meter. Most streets in San Francisco have some restriction or other. Many areas limit nonresident parking to two hours, some to one hour. Street cleaning happens weekly in some neighborhoods, three times a week in others.

When you park on a hill, city law requires you to curb your wheels. (Translation: When the car faces uphill, turn your wheel as far left as possible; when you park facing downhill, turn your wheel to the right. If you're parking on the left side of the street—on a one-way street, for instance—the opposite applies.) And just because you see cars parked on the sidewalk, don't assume it's legal.

Many curbs are color-coded, designating what kind of parking restrictions apply:

red	=	absolutely no parking or stopping
yellow	=	delivery truck loading zone from 7am to 6pm
white	=	picking up or dropping off passengers only
green	=	10- to 30-minute parking zone from 9am to 6pm
blue	=	disabled parking only; identification required

Follow these guidelines and, with a little forethought and a sense of humor, you'll find that driving through the city is a grand adventure.

PUBLIC TRANSPORTATION

San Franciscans are passionate about our public transportation system, Muni (the San Francisco Municipal Railway). Even though we love to make fun of how dreadful the service can be, we rely on its buses, streetcars, and cable cars to carry us from one end of town to another. And that they do, albeit in no hurry. Public transit is a good option for visitors who are not on a tight schedule. Although no single bus route follows the 49-Mile Drive exactly, several follow various parts of it, and some bus line or other goes close to almost every segment of the Drive. You'll find public transportation directions at the end of each segment of this book. If you plan to get around without a car, here are a few things to know:

Bus maps are available for sale at the Visitor Information Center on the mezzanine at Hallidie Plaza (Fifth and Market Streets). For a quick reference, the Pacific Bell Yellow Pages has a bus map.

Exact change only. Drivers do not carry change.

Muni's Passport offers unlimited rides on all Muni bus lines and cable cars. Passes come in a variety of time lengths. A one-day pass costs $6 and can be bought on any bus or cable car, and a three-day pass is $10. Either can be bought at the cable car turnaround at Fifth and Market (open every day, 8:30am to 8:30pm). A seven-day pass is $15 ($8 for seniors over 65 and children ages 5–17). These one-week passes start each Sunday, and they can be bought at the cable car turnaround and at all Safeway supermarkets.

If you're not using a pass and you'll be making a connection or returning within a couple of hours, ask the driver for a **transfer**. This slip of paper is good for two additional rides within the time marked at the bottom of the transfer. The first time you use it, the driver will tear off the top portion. The second time you use it, the driver is supposed to take the remaining piece (though often drivers never collect either piece).

Bus lines are numbered; streetcar lines are lettered. Cable car lines are named for the streets their routes follow—Hyde-Powell, California, and Powell-Mason. Buses with an L or an X after the number are express rush-hour buses that make limited stops.

Public transit after midnight is sparse. Consult bus maps posted at most stops, or call 415-673-MUNI (415-673-6864) for information.

Bay Area Rapid Transit, or **BART,** has eight stops in San Francisco. Most of those are along Market Street downtown and on Valencia Street in the Mission District. Call 650-992-BART (650-992-2278) for information.

WEATHER

In general, expect San Francisco to be a bit sunnier in spring and fall, foggy without rain in summer, and foggy and rainy in winter. That said, visitor beware! El Niño and La Niña years give us sunny winters and late rains—or is it foggy falls and floods in March? What we are trying to say is that San Francisco's climate is as changeable as a Giants' lineup card. Be ready for anything.

Nearly every neighborhood in the city has its own microclimate. The temperature in the eastern half of the city can easily be ten degrees higher than in the western end. Fog in one neighborhood may be deceiving; sun can lurk just on the other side of a hill. And cold winds along the water don't rule out a warm, still day in the middle of town. To add to the delightful confusion, the layer of fog that often covers the city at night usually burns off around midday, so what starts out as a cold, gray morning can turn into a gloriously bright afternoon. The best way to deal with the unpredictable nature of our climate is to prepare as San Franciscans do—wear layered clothing.

Alcatraz Island

San Francisco Bay

Treasure Island & Yerba Buena Island

San Francisco/ Oakland Bay Bridge

BAY BRIDGE

FERRY BLDG.

THE EMBARCADERO

SPEAR ST

BEALE ST

MAIN ST

STEUART ST

MARINA

COW HOLLOW

NORTH POINT ST

BAY ST

FORT MASON

FISHERMAN'S WHARF

BEACH ST

CHESTNUT ST

LOMBARD ST
GREENWICH ST

COIT TOWER

SCOTT ST

FILBERT ST
UNION ST

PACIFIC HEIGHTS

RUSSIAN HILL

NORTH BEACH

BAKER ST
BRODERICK ST
DIVISADERO ST

FILLMORE ST
WEBSTER ST

PACIFIC AVE
JACKSON ST

GREEN ST
VALLEJO ST
BROADWAY

CHINATOWN

COLUMBUS AVE

SANSOME ST
MONTGOMERY ST
BATTERY ST

LOCUST ST
LAUREL ST
WALNUT ST
PRESIDIO AVE

PINE ST
BUSH ST
SUTTER ST

SACRAMENTO ST

WASHINGTON ST
CLAY ST
CALIFORNIA ST

NOB HILL

TAYLOR
POWELL
GRANT
KEARNY ST

FINANCIAL DISTRICT

EUCLID AVE

GEARY

PIERCE ST
STEINER ST

POST ST
GEARY

UNION SQUARE

O'FARRELL ST

MISSION ST
HOWARD ST

1ST ST
2ND ST
3RD ST

ELLIS ST
EDDY ST

WESTERN ADDITION

LARKIN ST
HYDE ST
LEAVENWORTH ST
JONES ST

DOWNTOWN

TURK ST
GOLDEN GATE AVE
McALLISTER ST

CIVIC CENTER

MARKET ST

SOUTH OF MARKET

GROVE ST
HAYES ST
FELL ST

HAYES VALLEY

CITY HALL

OAK ST
PAGE ST
HAIGHT ST
WALLER ST

BUCHANAN ST
LAGUNA ST

GOUGH ST
FRANKLIN ST
12TH ST

9TH ST
10TH ST
8TH ST

FOLSOM ST

HARRISON ST

4TH ST
5TH ST

BRANNAN ST

KING ST

HAIGHT ASHBURY

DUBOCE

80

2ND ST
3RD ST

STATES

13TH ST

BRYANT ST

7TH ST

NOE ST
SANCHEZ ST
CHURCH ST

14TH ST
15TH ST
16TH ST
17TH ST

MISSION DOLORES

18TH ST

DOUGLAS ST
DIAMOND ST
CASTRO ST

CASTRO

19TH ST

20TH ST

21ST ST

SOUTH VAN NESS AVE
FOLSOM ST
HARRISON ST
FLORIDA ST

101

16TH ST

MISSION BAY

MARIPOSA ST

POTRERO HILL

DE HARO ST
WISCONSIN ST
CONNECTICUT ST

TEXAS ST
PENNSYLVANIA ST
TENNESSEE ST
ILLINOIS ST

DOLORES ST
GUERRERO ST
VALENCIA ST
MISSION ST

THE MISSION

YORK ST

POTRERO AVE

22ND ST

NOE VALLEY

27TH ST
28TH ST
29TH ST
30TH ST

24TH ST
25TH ST
26TH ST

CESAR CHAVEZ

101

3RD ST

25TH ST

280

SAN JOSE AVE

CESAR CHAVEZ

NAPOLEON ST

TOLAND ST

CARGO WAY

CORTLAND AVE

JARBOE AVE
TOMPKINS AVE
OGDEN AVE
CRESCENT

INDUSTRIAL

PALOU AVE
JERROLD AVE
QUINT ST
PHELPS ST

EVANS WAY

AVALON

SILVER

SWEENY

SILVER

NEWHALL ST
MENDELL ST

UNIVERSITY
HARVARD
CAMBRIDGE
ATHENS
MUNICH
MADISON

FELTON
BACON
WOOLSEY

GIRARD

280

101

THORNTON
SHAFTER
3RD ST
VAN DYKE

INNES

PRESIDIO BLVD
LINCOLN BLVD
RICHARDSON AVE
LYON ST

BOYLE DR

LOMBARD ST
VAN NESS AVE

PANKU AVE

COMPLETE DRIVING DIRECTIONS

The Drive starts at City Hall, mid-block of Dr. Carlton B. Goodlett Place (Polk Street between McAllister and Grove) facing south. Proceed to Grove Street and turn left (east). Turn left (north) at Larkin. Follow Larkin Street to Geary. Turn left (west) on Geary and continue to Gough Street.

Head west on Geary. The Japan Center is on your right. When you get to Webster Street, turn right (north), go one block, and turn right (east) again on Post Street. Follow Post for about 1 mile to reach Union Square, the grass-and-concrete plaza with palm trees on your right that begins at Powell Street. Continue on Post to Grant Avenue. Turn left (north) to Bush Street.

Drive north uphill through the Chinatown Gate two blocks to California Street. Turn left (west) onto California. Drive west on California four blocks to Taylor Street; turn right (north) onto Taylor and continue three blocks to Washington; turn right (east) onto Washington and continue two blocks to Powell Street. Turn right (south) onto Powell, proceed one block to Clay, turn left (east) onto Clay, and take it three blocks to Kearny. Portsmouth Square is on your left. Turn left (north) onto Kearny and drive one block to Washington.

Proceed north on Kearny to Columbus. Turn left onto Columbus (traveling northwest) and then, after a block, turn right (north) onto Grant Avenue. Follow Grant six blocks to Lombard Street. Turn left (west) onto Lombard and continue three blocks to Mason. Turn right (north) onto Mason and follow it six blocks to the waterfront.

Turn left (west) onto Jefferson Street. Follow Jefferson four blocks to Hyde Street. Turn left (south) onto Hyde and follow it one block to Beach Street. Turn right (west) onto Beach Street and continue two blocks to Polk Street. Turn left (south) onto Polk and proceed one block to Northpoint Street. Turn right (west) onto Northpoint and drive one block to Van Ness Avenue. Turn left (south) on Van Ness to Bay Street and turn right (west).

Follow Bay Street four blocks to Laguna; turn right (north) onto Laguna and left (west) two blocks later onto Beach Street. Bear right onto Marina Boulevard. Turn right (north) into the Marina Green parking area, curve around through the area, and turn left (south) at the small craft harbor entrance. Coming out of the parking area, continue straight ahead (south) on Scott Street two blocks to Beach Street. Turn right (west) onto Beach and follow it to its end (three blocks) at Baker Street. Turn left (south) onto Baker Street and drive two blocks to Bay Street; turn left (east) onto Bay, drive one block, and then turn right (south) onto Broderick. Turn right (west) onto Chestnut and cross the large boulevard called Richardson to reach Lyon (two blocks). Turn left (south) onto Lyon and drive one block to Lombard Street, to the entrance to the Presidio.

Turn right (west) from Lyon onto Lombard and drive through the Presidio entrance gate. The road curves right (northwest) and, after two blocks, joins Presidio Boulevard; it then veers right (north by northwest) and becomes Lincoln Boulevard. Turn left (south) onto Funston and follow it two blocks to Moraga. Turn right (west) onto Moraga and follow it five blocks to Infantry Terrace. Bear right (north) and go three blocks to merge with Lincoln Boulevard again. Stay left on Lincoln. With the exception of turnoffs for the National Cemetery, Fort Point, Golden Gate Bridge, and Baker Beach, stay on Lincoln until it exits the Presidio, becoming El Camino del Mar.

Continue west on El Camino del Mar, through Sea Cliff, and follow it into Lincoln Park (the first sign says "Land's End Recreation Area"). Turn left (south) and go past the Palace of the Legion of Honor on the right. Continue south to exit the park on 34th Avenue, and continue one block to Geary. Turn right (west) onto Geary; bear right to join Point Lobos Avenue at 42nd Avenue. Follow Point Lobos Avenue as it curves to the Cliff House.

From the Cliff House, continue downhill (south) for 4 miles. Bear right as the Great Highway merges with Skyline Boulevard. At John Muir Drive, turn left (southeast). Follow John Muir Drive to its end at Lake Merced Boulevard. Turn left (north) onto Lake Merced Boulevard and follow as it curves around the lake, past San Francisco State University, to a right-turn lane (north) at Sunset Boulevard. Follow the turn lane onto Sunset Boulevard and continue to its end at Martin Luther King Jr. Drive in Golden Gate Park.

Turn left (west) onto Martin Luther King Jr. Drive. Turn right (north) onto Chain of Lakes Drive (this is the first stop sign—the street is unmarked). Turn right (east) onto John F. Kennedy Drive. At the corner just before the underpass beneath 19th Avenue (the only one on John F. Kennedy Drive), turn right (south) onto Traverse Drive, and then at the next stop sign take a soft left (southeast) onto Middle Drive. Continue to the next stop sign, and turn left (east) onto Martin Luther King Jr. Drive. Cross 19th Avenue (through the traffic light) and continue to Stow Lake Drive. Turn left (north) onto Stow Lake Drive, and then turn right (east) just after the boathouse. This is Stow Lake Drive East, which curves around the lake. At its end, make a sharp left turn (east) onto Martin Luther King Jr. Drive. Follow it to Middle Drive, and then turn left (northeast). Where Middle Drive meets Lawn Bowling Drive, make a sharp right turn (south) and follow it to Martin Luther King Jr. Drive. Turn left (southeast) and continue to

Kezar Drive. Turn left (east) onto Kezar and stay to the right (east), continuing onto Waller Street. Follow Waller to Stanyan.

Turn right (south) from Waller onto Stanyan. At Parnassus (four blocks), turn right (west) and follow it seven blocks to 7th Avenue. Turn left (south) onto 7th Avenue, which becomes Laguna Honda. Continue on Laguna Honda, past the enormous retaining wall overlooking the reservoir, about 1.5 miles. At Woodside, turn left (east) for a half mile. At the top of the hill, turn left (northeast) onto Portola Drive. Almost immediately, there is a left-turn lane to Twin Peaks Boulevard. Take that left (north) onto a winding uphill road. Follow the sign at the top of the hill to the lookout point. When leaving the lookout area, turn right and right again to head downhill. Turn right (east) onto Clarendon. At Clayton, turn left (north), and then turn right (east) onto 17th Street. At Roosevelt, turn left (northeast), and continue to 14th Street. Turn right (east) onto 14th Street and head to the bottom of the hill to Market Street.

Cross Market Street on 14th Street eastbound, continue one block, and turn right (south) onto Dolores Street. Follow Dolores seventeen blocks to Cesar Chavez Street. Turn left (east) and follow it 2 miles to Indiana (just past the second freeway overpass). Turn left (north) onto Indiana to the northbound entrance to Interstate 280.

Enter Interstate 280 North and follow it to its end, where it becomes a city boulevard called King Street. Follow King Street northeast; where it curves to meet the shore, it becomes the Embarcadero. Continue along the Embarcadero to the Ferry Building.

Turn left (west) from the Embarcadero onto Washington Street. Follow it two blocks to Battery Street. Turn left (south) onto Battery and follow Battery to Bush Street. At Bush, bear left on Battery (all lanes can go left) and cross Market Street, where Battery becomes 1st Street. Follow 1st Street two blocks to Howard Street. Turn right (southwest) onto Howard Street and follow it to 9th Street. Turn right (north) on 9th, go two blocks, and as 9th crosses Market Street bear right onto Larkin; turn left (west) onto Grove and right (north) at Polk. The Drive ends at City Hall.

CIVIC CENTER

From City Hall to Cathedral Hill

CIVIC CENTER

City Hall and the Civic Center Plaza are the staging areas for the start of the 49-Mile Scenic Drive. From the City Hall Museum to the state-of-the-art public library, introduce yourself to the history and culture of the City by the Bay. The architectural grandeur will give you a glimpse of the vision of the "Rome of the Pacific" that was touted by the railroad and newspaper barons of the late nineteenth and early twentieth centuries.

From this center of western politics and culture, the great opera and symphony halls provide vivid contrast to the Tenderloin District's old and gritty apartment houses and stores, past which you will drive to reach Cathedral Hill, so called for its abundance of churches. A short detour will lead you along stately Van Ness Avenue, into the trendy, upbeat Hayes Valley neighborhood, or into the colorful outdoor market at United Nations Plaza.

BEST WAY TO VISIT

Most of the sights in this segment surround City Hall. We suggest that you park your car near Civic Center Plaza and visit the buildings in this area on foot.

The history museum in City Hall makes an excellent starting point—it will introduce you to many of the sights you'll visit during the rest of the 49-Mile Scenic Drive. After visiting the Civic Center area, drive the rest of the segment (street parking is available there, and Saint Mary's Cathedral has a parking lot). As in most cities, you should take extra care when walking at night. This area requires more caution than others.

THE DRIVE

1 CITY HALL San Francisco's City Hall is the center of local politics as well as one of the nation's finest examples of the Beaux-Arts style. Its central dome is taller than the Capitol dome in Washington, D.C. Arthur Brown Jr. designed City Hall in 1913, modeling it after Saint Peter's Basilica in Rome. The building opened in 1916, during Mayor James Rolph's reign.

City Hall was damaged during the 1989 earthquake and closed in 1995 for seismic retrofitting and remodeling. In 1999, it reopened after a $300 million facelift that included a refinished gold dome. Free and open to the public, City Hall houses the Museum of the City of San Francisco in the South Light Court. Actual street signs for the 49-Mile Scenic Drive are on sale at the SF Store in the North Light Court, where there is also a cafe. On the upper levels are the offices for the city supervisors and the mayor.

Both the interior and the exterior of City Hall have been used in many movies, among them *Jagged Edge* (1985), *Class Action* (1991), and *Tucker: The Man and His Dreams* (1988), as well as several of the Dirty Harry films.

The museum has two other nearby exhibit spaces as well: at the Earl Warren Judicial Center, 350 McAllister Street, and the Hiram Johnson State Building, 455 Golden Gate Avenue. (City Hall: Docent tour hotline 415/554-6023; open Monday to Friday 8am to 8pm, weekends 12pm to 4pm; Museum open Monday to Friday 9am to 5pm)

2 CIVIC CENTER PLAZA The heart of the Civic Center is its plaza. Originally conceived at the turn of the century as an "imperial" plaza in the French style for the burgeoning port city, it is the center of government and home to the city's most prestigious cultural institutions. Many chic restaurants catering to the politicians as well as to the symphony- and opera-goers in the vicinity are sprinkled throughout the surrounding streets. The same area is a favorite site of many political demonstrations and is frequently inhabited by the homeless.

On the south side of the Plaza is the Bill Graham Civic Auditorium— a hall used for concerts, parties, and ceremonies. Originally called Brooks Hall, the auditorium was renamed to honor the man who put San Francisco on the rock-and-roll map. Graham was the promoter of the great rock concerts of the 1960s, by groups such as the Jefferson Airplane, Big Brother and the Holding Company, and the Grateful Dead—and he continued to explore for new sounds until his death in 1991.

The Main Library, which opened in 1996, is the modern building on the southeast corner of the plaza, at Larkin and Grove. It features a number of specialty reading centers—the African American Center, Chinese Center, James C. Hormel Gay and Lesbian Center, Stegner Environmental Center, Herb Caen Magazine and Newspaper Center, Filipino-American Center, Silver Beach Blanket Babylon Music Center, Business Center, Jobs and Careers Center, Walker Patent and Trademark Center, Stern Book Art Center, San Francisco History Center, and Fisher Children's Center—in addition to its collection of 1.1 million books in more than fifty languages.

The rotating art exhibits in the glass cases on the sixth floor and in the Jewett Gallery on the lower level showcase everything from photography to children's art to historical artifacts. The library also hosts a multitude of free lectures, workshops, and video screenings. Schedules are available at the information desk, and many highlights are listed in the local newspapers.

Look on the sidewalk in front of the Bill Graham Civic Auditorium for the Bay Area Music Awards Walk of Fame. Seven bronze plaques embedded in the pavement on Grove Street pay tribute to some of San Francisco's greatest musicians: Jefferson Airplane, John Lee Hooker, Carlos Santana, Jerry Garcia, Janis Joplin, and Metallica, as well as the man who made it all possible, Bill Graham.

The Main Library opened on April 18, 1996—the ninetieth anniversary of the great quake—and was designed by I. M. Pei, the same architect who designed the controversial pyramid in front of the Louvre in Paris.

The word "new" is often attached to this library's name because it was built to replace what's now known as the old Main Library at 200 Larkin Street on the corner of McAllister. This building, the original central library, opened in 1917 and quickly became inadequate for the vast number of San Franciscans who used it each day. However, it wasn't until 1988 that voters approved a bond to build a new library—the first in a series of projects to revive the Civic Center to its turn-of-the-century glory. Of course, most of the other renovations were inspired by the damage sustained during the 1989 Loma Prieta earthquake, but even before the earthquake struck, a strong desire to improve the Civic Center permeated the city's consciousness.

The historic yet empty old Main Library is now being renovated and will reopen in June 2002 as the new home of the Asian Art Museum (currently located adjacent to the de Young Museum in Golden Gate Park; see the Golden Gate Park segment for its description).

3 **UNITED NATIONS PLAZA** Barely off the Drive is United Nations Plaza (Fulton Street at Hyde Street, behind the Main Library), designed as a memorial to the drafting and signing of the United Nations Charter in San Francisco in 1945. The Heart of the City Farmers' Market is held here every Sunday and Wednesday morning, bringing fresh produce, flowers, and prepared meals, along with thousands of people, to the area.

4 **VAN NESS AVENUE** Although not actually on the 49-Mile Drive route, three buildings on Van Ness Avenue, along the western side of City Hall, play vital parts in San Francisco history and culture:

- **Davies Symphony Hall** (201 Van Ness Avenue at Grove Street). Built in 1980, this 2,700-seat, glass-and-concrete structure is the home of the San Francisco Symphony and host to visiting performance groups.

- **War Memorial Opera House** (301 Van Ness Avenue at Grove Street). The San Francisco Opera (fall) and the San Francisco Ballet (winter and spring) perform in this nearly 3,200-seat hall. Built in 1932, the opera house is the centerpiece of the performing-arts complex around City Hall. After World War II, the peace treaty between Japan and the United States was signed in this building.

As you pass Turk Street heading north on Larkin, make like a local and look for the quirky quote of the month on the marquee of the Kahn-Keville car shop on the northwest corner.

- **Veteran's Memorial Building** (401 Van Ness Avenue at McAllister). This building, once the home of the San Francisco Museum of Modern Art (now located in the South of Market area; see the Downtown and South of Market segment), was built early in the century. In 1945, the United Nations Charter was signed here. Today it houses the Performing Arts Library and Museum (PALM), a venue for exhibits on the Bay Area performing arts. Also here is the Herbst Theatre, built in 1932, a 900-seat hall used for chamber concerts and other small-venue performances. The San Francisco Municipal Railway and other city agencies use the rest of the building for administrative offices.

5 **HAYES VALLEY** This charming neighborhood just west of Van Ness Avenue between Market and Grove Streets is a fairly recent development in San Francisco's landscape. The Central Freeway, looming over nearby Octavia Street, was damaged in the 1989 earthquake. The city closed the Oak Street entrance, and since then a quaint merchant strip has blossomed in what was once a run-down neighborhood in the shadow of a freeway overpass.

This part of Hayes Street, between Franklin on the east and Laguna on the west, has enjoyed a sprucing up, with many cafes, salons, and boutiques moving in. Seafood lovers will enjoy the upscale **Hayes Street Grill** (324 Hayes St; 415/863-5545). For more of the flavor of the original

Dashiell Hammett, the acclaimed mystery writer of the 1920s and 1930s, lived, loved, and wrote in a number of sites around the City Hall area. Besides visiting the old Main Library (200 Larkin) almost daily, "Dash" lived in an apartment at 620 Eddy Street (between Larkin and Polk Streets) and later in another at 891 Post (on the corner of Hyde Street). Much of the action in his books takes place in real buildings throughout this area. For instance, you can still faintly see the sign for Blanco's Restaurant (between Polk and Larkin on Olive Street), which figured in *The Dain Curse*. Fans can take a fee-based tour of Hammett locales during June only. Meet on the corner of Fulton and Larkin Streets (in front of the Main Library) at noon on those Saturdays. For more information, call 510/287-9540.

neighborhood, visit **Powell's Place** (511 Hayes Street; 415/863-1404), a soul food restaurant opened in 1977 by local gospel legend Emmit Powell.

DIRECTIONS

DRIVING

The Drive starts at City Hall, mid-block of Dr. Carlton B. Goodlett Place (Polk Street between McAllister and Grove) facing south. Proceed to Grove Street and turn left (east). Turn left (north) at Larkin. Follow Larkin Street to Geary. Turn left (west) on Geary and continue to Gough Street. (See page 22 for continued driving directions.)

PARKING

Public parking is available in the garage below the Civic Center Plaza, in front of City Hall, and in the Performing Arts Public Garage on Grove between Franklin and Gough Streets, behind the Opera House. Metered street parking is available as well.

BUS

To start on the Drive from City Hall, catch the 42–Downtown Loop, 47–Van Ness, or 49–Van Ness–Mission on Van Ness, heading north, and get off at Geary. Walk two blocks uphill (west) on Geary to Gough Street, or catch the 38-Geary at the corner of Van Ness and ride the two blocks to the ending point of this segment (Geary at Gough Street). (See page 22 for continued bus directions.)

WALKING

In this segment, walkers should follow the driving directions.

JAPANTOWN &
UNION SQUARE

From Saint Mary's Cathedral to the French Quarter

JAPANTOWN & UNION SQUARE

From the highly modern Saint Mary's Cathedral atop Cathedral Hill, the Drive takes you west on a major thoroughfare, Geary. At the bottom of the hill, you'll reach Japan Center—a great spot to grab some sushi, buy an antique kimono, or drop into a Japanese spa—in the historic Western Addition neighborhood. As you head back downtown, you'll see the varied architecture of lower Pacific Heights—with everything from Victorian row houses to Shinto temples to original Julia Morgan designs. Farther east on the eclectic and newly revitalized stretch of Post Street, the Drive takes you past mystery writer Dashiell Hammett's former home and then a sprinkling of coffee shops, art galleries, and

Southeast Asian restaurants amid the large apartment buildings. At Union Square, a palm-lined plaza surrounded by fancy department stores and high-class hotels, you'll be in the commercial center of downtown San Francisco. From here, a short detour will lead you to a Frank Lloyd Wright building on Maiden Lane or into the city's celebrated French Quarter.

BEST WAY TO VISIT

This segment is easy to drive. When you get to Union Square, however, the streets become extremely congested. You may want to park your car at one of the garages under or around Union Square and stroll the area on foot.

Because downtown burned in the great fire after the 1906 earthquake, most of the older residences in this area are west of Van Ness Avenue. We have included in the Architecture of Lower Pacific Heights description (see below) some of the locations of nineteenth-century houses. It will mean going off the Drive, but the detour is well worth it to those interested in the time period. Farther away from the Drive but still in the Western Addition is Alamo Square, of postcard fame. Although it is out of the way, the square has one of those picturesque views that define San Francisco.

THE DRIVE

1 SAINT MARY'S CATHEDRAL There have been three Saint Mary's churches and cathedrals in San Francisco. The first, downtown and known as Old Saint Mary's Church, is still standing and active at California Street and Grant Avenue (see Saint Mary's Square and Old Saint Mary's Church in the Chinatown and Nob Hill segment). The 1887 Saint Mary's on Van Ness, a large red-brick structure, burned to the ground in 1962. Replacing it at 1111 Gough Street is the new Saint Mary's Cathedral, which was completed in 1971.

This recent addition to the unusual buildings of San Francisco is a concrete, travertine, and glass structure that rises above two blocks of Cathedral Hill. The frame rises to an equilateral cross. The abstract designs in the stained glass represent fire (west), water (east), sky (north), and earth (south). Some people were critical of the building when it was erected, but its unusual form has come to be recognized as one of San Francisco's signature oddities. *San Francisco Chronicle* columnist Herb Caen said that it looked like the agitator of a Maytag washing machine.

The interior is an enormous open space rising 190 feet. Views of the city can be had from the southern corners, both east and west, and on its north side is the great organ. The priest conducts mass for up to 2,500 people from an austere (for Roman Catholic cathedrals) altar on the south side, over which is a canopy-like sculpture of aluminum rods that, as the air moves its pieces, shimmers light on the altar and the congregation. *(1111 Gough Street at Geary; 415/567-2020)*

If you want to visit the cathedral, you have two choices for parking. You can park on Geary near Gough Street and cross Geary on foot. Feed the meter! After your visit, return to the car and proceed down Geary. Or, to park in the cathedral's parking lot, you'll have to go around the block: proceed on Geary to Laguna and make a right turn (north); at Post, make another right (east), and then another right (south) at Gough; cross Geary, and turn right into the parking lot. To leave the church parking lot and return to the Drive, exit to the west, turning left (south) on Cleary, and follow it to Laguna. Turn right (north) on Laguna and then left (west) on Geary.

2 **JAPANTOWN** The northeast section of the Western Addition, first built in the 1850s for European immigrants, became the home for tens of thousands of Issei (Japan-born immigrants) in the early 1900s. (For a more detailed description of the Western Addition, see below.) The original 40-block area was vacated when all Japanese—

The New Chicago Barber Shop (1551 Fillmore Street, near Geary) has a long history in the neighborhood. When it opened in 1952, this family-run barber shop was located at Fillmore and Ellis Streets. It has been at Fillmore and Geary since 1968. Many prominent San Franciscans get their hair cut here, including Glide Memorial's Reverend Cecil Williams and Mayor Willie Brown.

both Issei and U.S.-born—were interned by Executive Order 9066 of President Roosevelt.

African Americans from many southern states who moved to San Francisco to work in the local war industries took up residence in the then-vacated Japantown. After the war, having no community to return to, many of San Francisco's freed Japanese Americans settled in other areas of the city. Today, citizens of Japanese descent live throughout the Bay Area. Yet Japantown is still home to about 12,000 people of Japanese ancestry.

In the 1960s, urban renewal took down most of Japantown's older structures, including many Victorian buildings that needed remodeling, and replaced them with modern buildings with Japanese-style façades. The Japanese Cultural and Trade Center, more commonly called the Japan Center, opened in 1968. It is the centerpiece of Japantown and features a 35-store shopping mall, an underground garage, a hotel, movie theaters, a Japanese-style bathhouse, and restaurants. Even if you don't like malls, Japantown is probably worth a stop. Its exotic array of shops—try Kinokuniya for books and Mikado Hardware for kitchen goods—makes it far from a typical mall.

In the Peace Plaza at Buchanan and Post Streets stands the Peace Pagoda, a gift from Japan. This 100-foot-high multilevel structure rises from a reflecting pool on pillars to five copper roofs and then continues to a spire upon which sits a golden ball. It was designed by Yoshiro Taniguchi of Tokyo, who adapted it from the design of the 1,200-year-old Pagoda of Eternal Peace in Nara, Japan. Recently renovated, the Peace Pagoda creates a cohesive center to Japantown.

One of Japantown's oldest businesses is still standing—the Uoki Market (1656 Post Street) opened in 1906 as a fish market. Three generations later, it is still run by the Sakai family, selling fresh fish and other culinary staples to the now highly assimilated Japanese community.

WESTERN ADDITION AND THE FILLMORE OVERVIEW

At the corner of Geary and Fillmore are two of San Francisco's legendary musical institutions. On the northwest corner stands John Lee Hooker's blues club, the **Boom Boom Room**. On the southwest corner is the historic **Fillmore Auditorium**, the launching pad for the careers of many 1960s rock bands, not the least of which were the Grateful Dead, Paul Butterfield Blues Band, the Jefferson Airplane, and Quicksilver Messenger Service.

North on Fillmore Street is **Lower Pacific Heights**, facetiously called "Baja Pac Heights" by locals. Although this area is technically part of the Western Addition, the inflated real estate prices of the 1990s drove new residents to associate more with their wealthy neighbors to the north than with their working- and middle-class neighbors to the south. The rule of thumb in San Francisco is that as the hills get higher, so does the wealth of their dwellers. If you continue north on Fillmore Street, you'll be in the very posh Pacific Heights neighborhood.

If you head south, you'll be in the Fillmore—known as the Fillmo' or the Mo'—a corridor in the larger neighborhood known as the Western Addition. The term "Western Addition" originally referred to everything built west of Van Ness Avenue in 1870, including the smaller areas we now call Pacific Heights and Japantown. Nowadays, Western Addition refers more specifically to the area between Van Ness Avenue and Broderick Street and between Fell Street and Geary. The area was first settled by Jewish and Japanese immigrants, followed by African Americans, who moved in when the Japanese were interned during World War II. After the war, when naval dockyards and munitions factories closed and commercial shipping moved to Oakland, the predominantly black community was left unemployed.

With today's economic prosperity and residential movement back to the city, ethnic diversity is increasing in the Western Addition. Efforts have been made to restore black-owned businesses along lower Fillmore Street by developing a "jazz district" in a place that was once famous for its innovative music scene.

Small clubs have recently sprung up. In addition to John Lee Hooker's Boom Boom Room, check out **Rasselas** (1534 Fillmore Street) and **Someplace Else** (1795 Geary) for local jazz and blues. Many shops and organizations owned by and catering to their African American neighbors line the southern ends of Divisadero and Fillmore Streets.

Many postcard photos have been shot at **Alamo Square,** the most pristine corner of the Western Addition. From the large grassy hill bounded by Hayes, Fulton, Steiner, and Scott (admittedly quite a ways off the Drive), you look out on a row of exquisite "painted ladies," as San Francisco's colorful Victorian houses are called, with a backdrop of the city skyline. Alamo Square is equally great for a relaxing picnic or a romp with the kids or your dog.

3 ARCHITECTURE OF LOWER PACIFIC HEIGHTS The area just north of Japan Center, know as Lower (or "Baja," the Spanish word for lower) Pacific Heights, reflects in its architecture the varied religious, ethnic, and aesthetic influences that have shaped the neighborhood over the years. From the European styles of the nineteenth century to the Japanese and American tastes of the twentieth century, the buildings in this area make for a fascinating visual history of the city. (For a more extended guide to San Francisco's architectural history, visit the **Haas-Lilienthal House Museum** at 2007 Franklin Street. The Queen Anne–style mansion built in 1886 is now the museum of the Foundation for San Francisco's Architectural History.)

Just two blocks off the drive is a picturesque row of houses that exemplify the European influences on San Francisco architectural styles of the nineteenth century. On the block of Laguna between Bush and Pine, you will find six Eastlake or Stick Style houses (the even-numbered buildings) built in 1889 by William Hinkel; on the other side of the street (the odd-numbered addresses) are eleven Italianate row houses built in 1877.

Reflecting the changing face of the neighborhood during the twentieth century, the area around Japan Center is now filled with temples and community centers catering to the Japanese. Among them are the **Konko Church of San Francisco** (1901 Bush Street, at the corner of Laguna), a Shinto temple built in 1973 with services in Japanese. The **Soto Zen Mission Sokoji** (1691 Laguna Street at Sutter) is a Buddhist temple that was built in 1984. Its minimalist interior is designed to encourage meditation. The **Nichi Bei Kai Cultural Center** (1759 Sutter Street) sits on a block of Victorian-style houses. The three-story building has a small Japanese garden and a special room, made of all natural materials, for performing the tea ceremony.

Famed California architect Julia Morgan designed the home for the **Western Addition YWCA** at 1830 Sutter Street. This building mixes the Craftsman style with Japanese design. Next door, at 1840 Sutter Street, is the **Japanese Cultural and Community Center**. Designed by Wayne Osaki in 1987, its stucco-and-wood exterior and brown-tiled roof hold meeting rooms and a senior center. A group of community organizations own the building and have established a mission "to preserve and transmit to future generations the Nikkei community's unique history and heritage."

4 POST STREET AND THE TENDER NOB Once you cross Van Ness Avenue, Post Street takes on a unique identity. Too low on the hill to technically be considered part of Nob Hill, the street is also too far north of the Tenderloin to qualify as a legitimate piece of that neighborhood. Because of its neither-here-nor-there locale, San Franciscans today dub this area "the Tender Nob." This strip of Post Street has seen tremendous change during the 1990s. What was once a somewhat seedy yet bustling residential street is now booming with cafes, South and Southeast Asian restaurants, and art galleries.

As you approach Hyde Street, look to your right. On the southeast corner at 891 Post is an apartment building that was the former home of Dashiell Hammett. According to the book *The Dashiell Hammett Tour*, by Don Herron, not only did Hammett create the character of Sam Spade, the iconoclastic detective of *The Maltese Falcon*, here, but Spade also "lived" in this apartment building. According to the book, Spade tells Joel Cairo, "This is Spade. Can you come up to my place—Post Street—now?" By following other descriptions later in the text, Hammett sleuths have placed Spade in the apartment on the fourth floor overlooking Post, where Hammett lived.

5 **THEATER DISTRICT** Like many San Francisco neighborhoods, the theater district represents a real cross-section of cultures. Nestled between the Union Square shopping area and the seedy Tenderloin, the theaters here feature shows ranging from *Phantom of the Opera* to "Live! Nude! Girls!" San Francisco's theatrical tradition dates back to the gold rush era; the **Alcazar Theater** (650 Geary) is the last remaining company of this time.

Scattered around the intersection of Geary and Mason you'll find the city's premier theaters: the **Geary Theater** (415 Geary) houses the highly esteemed **American Conservatory Theater** (ACT) troupe; the **Curran Theatre** (445 Geary) features Broadway plays and musicals; the **Theater on the Square** (450 Post Street) shows an eclectic mix of performances; the **Cable Car Theater** (430 Mason Street) is home to *Tony and Tina's Wedding*, a show in which the actors perform an elaborate wedding and the audience is made a part of the show as the wedding guests.

The **Lorraine Hansberry Theatre** (620 Sutter Street) is considered by some to be the best African American theater organization in the State of California. The **Marines Memorial Theatre** (609 Sutter Street) was one of the two original theaters to host the ACT (the other was the Geary) when it first came to San Francisco in the 1960s.

A bit further away but equally important to the local acting scene are the **Golden Gate Theatre** (1 Taylor Street, at Market), which housed the Broadway hit *Rent* in 1999, and the **Orpheum Theatre** (1192 Market Street), which featured vaudeville when it opened during the roaring '20s and now showcases big Broadway musicals such as *Showboat* and *Hello, Dolly*.

6 GLIDE MEMORIAL CHURCH Lively and dramatic, in keeping with its theater-district location, Glide Memorial celebrates an only-in-San-Francisco kind of holiness. The hundreds of worshippers (sometimes as many as 1,500) who gather here on Sunday mornings include believers of all stripes—gay, lesbian, and transgender, recovering addicts, and the homeless, as well as a vast array of the plain old curious.

The Reverend Cecil Williams and his wife, Janice Murikatani, are active community members—well known for their food program, drug counseling, shelter, and children's center. It comes as no surprise that the message at Glide is about restoring the human spirit and achieving social justice. But that isn't all there is to it. The gospel service often includes live jazz and a psychedelic slide show in addition to the lively singing; it starts at 9am every Sunday. *(330 Ellis Street; 415/771-6300; www.glide.org)*

7 UNION SQUARE Union Square is the heart of downtown. A rectangular hole amidst the skyscrapers of San Francisco, the square is an established local meeting place and tourist destination, a regular happening of people and events. Its name derives from its role as the site of pro-Union–Civil War rallies in the early 1860s. Later, to commemorate the naval battle at Manila Bay in the Spanish-American War, an obelisk-like column known as the Dewey Monument was erected in Union Square. Atop the granite structure is a sculpture of Victory, whose model was a major philanthropist in her time.

The Union Square area is San Francisco's version of shopping heaven. Located between Powell and Stockton Streets and between Geary and Post Streets, this grass-and-concrete park reflects the pulse of downtown San Francisco. Tony stores line three of the streets facing Union Square,

Tickets are available at box offices at the theaters, or at the Tix Area Box Office discount booth on Union Square, Stockton Street between Geary and Post. The Tix booth sells theater tickets for 50 percent of the regular price when you purchase them the day of the show, or for the full price when they are bought in advance. Credit-card payment is accepted only for the full-price advance tickets; for the half-price tickets, be prepared with cash or traveler's checks. Tix is open 11am to 6pm Tuesday through Thursday and 11am to 7pm Friday and Saturday. It is closed on Sunday and Monday.

Post Street was once known as "Club Row" because of the many social clubs located there in the 1920s: the Olympic Club, Bohemian Club, Union League, and Elks Club.

including high-class department stores and the fashion boutiques of top-name designers.

Some of San Francisco's finest hotels, restaurants, and shopping are around or near the square. The Westin Saint Francis Hotel, built in 1904 and reconstructed in 1906, is on the western side of the square; lunch or tea in its bar, the Compass Rose, is an elegant way to spend part of the afternoon. Macy's dominates the south side of the square. Smaller, more exclusive shops, such as Giorgio Armani and Alfred Dunhill, line the northern side, with Saks Fifth Avenue as their anchor. On the east are stores such as Lily Samii Collection and Hermes of Paris. Neiman-Marcus faces the southeast corner at Geary and Stockton; originally the City of Paris department store, that building is almost completely gone, except for the four-story rotunda and its signature emblem, the sailing ship, on its dome, which were worked into the new building's structure.

8 MAIDEN LANE AND THE CIRCLE GALLERY BUILDING Just off Union Square to the east is Maiden Lane, a pedestrian street of exclusive shops and important architecture. Originally a wild and bawdy street of bars and brothels called Morton Street, its name was changed when the bordellos were closed and the area was cleaned up for more "legitimate" businesses.

The building at **140 Maiden Lane** is considered one of the most important architectural works in the city. This Frank Lloyd Wright–designed restructure of a 1911 edifice was once known as the V. C. Morris Building and is now called the **Circle Gallery**. It is thought to be an architectural study for Wright's design of the Guggenheim Museum in New York City.

9 **FRENCH QUARTER** The small neighborhood tucked between Union Square, Chinatown, and the Financial District took on its French character in the early 1990s, and as yet it has no official name. Known most commonly as the French Quarter, it is also called Little Paris and the French Ghetto.

Al Jolson, famed singer and actor, died while playing a game of poker in the Saint Francis Hotel.

With the **French Consulate** (540 Bush Street), the **Notre Dame des Victoires Church** (566 Bush Street), and a slew of French cafes and bistros in an area of just two blocks, the *quartier* has become headquarters for the Bay Area's 30,000 to 40,000 French citizens and countless American Francophiles. The best time to soak up the lively spirit of this neighborhood is the night of July 14, when thousands come out to celebrate Bastille Day and party as if they themselves had won the French Revolution.

No matter when you visit the French Quarter, don't miss these spots: **Cafe de la Presse** (corner of Bush and Grant, across the street from the Chinatown Gate), a bustling sidewalk cafe, houses a vast selection of newspapers and magazines from around the world. Dating from the early 1970s, **Le Central** (453 Bush Street) is practically an antique establishment for this neighborhood of nouveaux riches. The somewhat rustic French brasserie was a favorite of columnist Herb Caen and is frequented by Mayor Willie Brown.

Just around the corner, **Claude Lane** (between Bush and Sutter and Kearny and Grant) is a quiet alley closed to car traffic. On it are the charming **Cafe Claude** (a great place to catch live jazz or sip an apéritif) and the fashionable boutique of local clothing designer Diana Slavin.

At the corner of Bush and Belden Place (east of Kearney) stands **Sam's Grill and Seafood Restaurant** (374 Bush Street)—not a French restaurant, but a classic San Francisco joint that dates from 1867. It marks the entrance to **Belden Place** (between Bush and Pine and between Kearny and Montgomery) another pedestrian-only alleyway—that is, if you can maneuver around the crowds of people at outdoor tables. With two French restaurants— Plouf Seafood Bistro (40 Belden Place) and Cafe Bastille (22 Belden Place)— as well as three non-French restaurants, a sunny lunch hour or a rare warm evening on this gastronomic strip is sure to please diners of every taste — especially those who enjoy being served by flirtatious French waiters.

DIRECTIONS

DRIVING

To continue the Drive from the previous segment (Geary at Gough): Head west on Geary. The Japan Center is on your right. When you get to Webster Street, turn right (north), go one block, and turn right (east) again on Post Street. Follow Post for about 1 mile to reach Union Square, the grass-and-concrete plaza with palm trees on your right that begins at Powell Street. Continue on Post to Grant Avenue. Turn left (north) to Bush Street. (See page 33 for continued driving directions.)

PARKING

Street parking is available around Japan Center, most of it at one-hour paid meters with a two-hour limit for nonresidents. Off-street parking is available underneath the Kabuki Theater in Japan Center. Enter on Geary or Post. A third entrance is one block west of the Drive on Fillmore.

Around Union Square, street parking is very difficult. Park in the underground parking garage beneath the square, which you can enter from Post or Geary, or in the Sutter-Stockton parking garage a block north. An additional public lot is the Ellis-O'Farrell Garage.

BUS

Walk downhill (west) on Geary to Webster Street and explore the Japan Center. Then catch the 2–Clement on Post at Webster heading east. Get off at Union Square, at the corner of Post and Powell Streets. Walk east two blocks to Grant; turn left (north) onto Grant and walk one block to Bush Street. (See page 34 for continued bus directions.)

WALKING

Geary is a major thoroughfare for car traffic, so it's not a quaint street for a stroll. However, the sidewalks are wide and the grade is downhill, so it makes for a fairly comfortable walk nonetheless. In this segment, walkers should follow the driving directions.

CHINATOWN & NOB HILL

From the Chinatown Gate to Portsmouth Square

CHINATOWN & NOB HILL

You'll feel the bustle of Chinatown as soon as you pass the foo dogs at the Chinatown Gate and begin your trek uphill on Grant Avenue, San Francisco's oldest street. Traffic here may be slow, because the street maintains its original skinny width dating from 1839. But this will give you time to look above the chock-a-block gift stores for a glimpse of the "chinoiserie" architectural details—a sort of East-meets-West aesthetic—that characterize the neighborhood.

The Drive turns onto California Street to follow the cable cars up a very steep hill, atop which is the fashionable Nob Hill neighborhood, former home of the great railroad "robber barons" of the late nineteenth century. After circling the world-famous hotels that stand there now, the Drive descends back into Chinatown, passing the Cable Car Barn and Museum, which houses the huge wheel towing the entire system's cables. It then proceeds on to the colorful shops selling everything from electronic trinkets to silk pajamas and porcelain figurines; markets with seasoned duck, pork buns, and live fish;

tea shops with herbal powders to cure any ailment; magazine kiosks with Asian-language publications; and restaurants galore. As you make your way through this lively neighborhood (be sure to check out the Chinese characters on the public street signs), you'll realize that Chinatown isn't just a neighborhood—it's practically a city all its own. This segment of the Drive ends at Portsmouth Square, San Francisco's oldest public plaza and the birthplace of the gold rush.

BEST WAY TO VISIT

Because driving and parking in the downtown area are difficult, we recommend that you park in a public garage near Union Square, Saint Mary's Square, or Portsmouth Square. Since there are steep hills on this route, we also recommend that you use public transportation where walking can be a challenge.

Both this segment of the Drive and the North Beach segment cover rich and scenic territory. You could easily take a full day to explore these few miles. If you're so inclined, we recommend that you park your car at the Sutter-Stockton garage and tackle Chinatown, Nob Hill, and North Beach on foot. When you've reached the end of the North Beach segment at the northern waterfront, catch the Powell-Mason cable car at Taylor and Bay for a ride back over the hill. Get off at Powell and Sutter. A short walk one block east on Sutter will bring you back to the Sutter-Stockton garage.

Adding the Northern Waterfront: Fisherman's Wharf to the day's sightseeing is another good way to expand this route. (See the next segment for details.) When you've reached the end of Fisherman's Wharf near Ghirardelli Square, catch the Powell-Hyde cable car at Hyde and Beach Streets for a ride back over the hill.

THE DRIVE

1 **CHINATOWN GATE** Spanning Grant Avenue at Bush Street, the ornate entrance to Chinatown welcomes visitors to the area. The gate was designed by Clayton Lee and was constructed in 1970. Following the tenets of *feng shui*, a Chinese aesthetic philosophy that connects physical space with spiritual well-being, the gate faces south, considered the most hospitable direction from which to enter a city or building.

Atop the gate are dragons that represent power and fertility. The fish below represent prosperity, while the mythological foo dogs are the gate's guards, protecting the community from evil spirits. The inscription is a quote from Dr. Sun Yat-Sen, the leader of the Chinese democratic revolution early in the last century. It states, "All under heaven is for the good of the people."

2 **SAINT MARY'S SQUARE AND OLD SAINT MARY'S CHURCH** Just east of the corner of Grant Avenue and California Street is Saint Mary's Square. In its small park is a statue of Dr. Sun Yat-Sen. In 1910, Dr. Sun lived in Chinatown, where he formed the political party that later became the Kuomintang, which led the fight in the teens to depose the royalty of China. Commissioned in 1938, the statue was created by Beniamino Bufano. The park also contains a plaque honoring Chinese Americans who lost their lives in the two World Wars.

The oldest of the three San Francisco churches named for Saint Mary, the church that gives its name to this square was dedicated in 1854. In Chinese it is called *Dai Choong Low*, or Tower of the Big Bell. In the mid-to-late nineteenth century, the church stood in contrast to the brothels and dance halls lining Grant Avenue (then called Dupont). It took a major earth-shaking to dislodge the brothels, but the church continues to this day. Stop in for a look at its interior.

The Drive leaves Chinatown here for Nob Hill. After this detour through a bit of old-wealth San Francisco, the Drive returns to the heart of Chinatown.

3 **NOB HILL** Whether you're clicking your heels across the marble floors of the Fairmont Hotel or walking your poodle through Huntington Park, it's pretty clear why locals call Nob Hill "Snob Hill." The stylish little hilltop has a long history of lodging San Francisco's gentry; now home to the city's most opulent hotels, it's become the resting spot for the wealthy from around the world.

The advent of cable cars in the 1870s made Nob Hill accessible to development for the first time. Men who made millions mining silver in Nevada or building the Southern Pacific Railroad had their mansions built on the top of the hill. Among the "robber barons" (so called for their predatory approaches to business) settling on Nob Hill were the railroad industry's Big Four: Charles Crocker, Collis P. Huntington, Leland Stanford, and Mark Hopkins.

The history of Huntington Park, set almost as the centerpiece of the area at the corner of California and Taylor, is emblematic of the dramatic politics of the railroad baron era. It was here that David Colton—a lawyer for the Southern Pacific Railroad and a minority partner of the Big Four—built his mansion.

Upon Colton's death, a huge embezzlement scandal ensued. Colton's estate was sued by the Southern Pacific Railroad Company, and his widow responded by making public detailed correspondence between her husband and Collis P. Huntington. In her attempt to prove that the Big Four had in fact embezzled millions during the building of the railroad, Mrs. Colton revealed Huntington's letters explaining the under-the-table deals he was cutting with Washington politicians.

But the drama didn't end there. Mrs. Colton sold the mansion in 1880, only to have it purchased in 1892 by Huntington himself. Like the rest of the property atop Nob Hill, the Colton/Huntington mansion was destroyed in the great fire that followed the earthquake of 1906. Huntington's widow donated the land to the city in 1915; it remains today as one of the few public areas on Nob Hill.

After the Nob Hill mansions burned down in 1906, classy hotels sprouted in their places. The Stanford Court Hotel (905 California Street) stands on what was once Leland Stanford's estate. The Mark Hopkins Hotel (1 Nob Hill Circle, on the southeast corner of Mason and California Streets) was built on the site of Mark Hopkins's burned-out mansion. Stop in at the Top of the Mark restaurant for a 360-degree panoramic view of the city. The hotel was featured in *Bullitt* (1968), *Sudden Impact* (1983), and *Innerspace* (1987).

The first Fairmont Hotel was built in 1902 by Tessie Fair, daughter of silver magnate James G. Fair. It was completed just days before the 1906 earthquake, but—a victim of the fire—it didn't open until a full year later. The hotel was immediately rebuilt under the supervision of architect Julia Morgan in 1907. The Fairmont Plunge—its terrace-level swimming pool— was inaugurated by actress Helen Hayes in the 1920s. In the late 1940s, the hotel was redecorated by Dorothy Draper in a rococo style with a dark palette. It was renovated in 1999 to enhance Julia Morgan's original design, with more natural light and a color scheme of cream and gold. *(northeast corner of California and Mason Streets; 415/772-5000)*

The Huntington Hotel (1075 California Street) is something of a museum of nineteenth-century Nob Hill. Although it dates from 1924, the hotel houses an impressive collection of old photographs as well as a historic restaurant—aptly named the Big Four.

On the western side of Huntington Park stands Grace Cathedral (1100 California Street; 415/749-6300), built on the site of the mansions of Charles and William Crocker. When their property was reduced to ash in 1906, the Crockers donated the land to the Episcopal Church.

Work began in 1928 to build a church in the style of Notre Dame in Paris, and it was completed in 1964. Instead of stone, the material used in the French cathedral, Grace Cathedral is built of concrete and steel to assure greater stability during earthquakes. The rose window was made in Chartres. The bronze doors, showing scenes from the Old Testament, are replicas of Ghiberti's *Gates of Paradise* in the Cathedral Baptistery of San Giovanni in Florence.

Inside the church, visitors are invited to follow a floor tapestry labyrinth, symbolizing the spiritual journey. In the north tower is the AIDS Interfaith

Cable cars were unknown to San Franciscans when Hallidie built the first line in 1873, which ran down Clay Street to Portsmouth Square. When the time came for the first test of the cable car along Clay, the designated driver looked down the track and, seeing the steepness of the descent, panicked, believing that the ride was certain death. Andrew Hallidie himself took over and guided the cable car down for the first time.

Chapel with an altarpiece by Keith Haring. *(open daily 7am to 5:45pm; guided tours are available Monday through Friday 1 to 3pm, Saturday 11:30am to 1:30pm, and Sunday 12:30 to 2pm)*

In the middle of "Snob Hill" stands the ultimate justification of that nickname—the Pacific Union Club (1000 California Street)—a highly selective social club for wealthy men. The Renaissance-style brownstone mansion was built in 1885 for "Silver King" James Clair Flood. Because it was made of stone, it was the only building on Nob Hill to survive the 1906 disaster. The club bought it and hired Willis Polk in 1908 to redecorate the interior. Since it opened in 1911, the club has permitted women to enter on only two occasions.

4 CABLE CAR BARN AND MUSEUM When first developed in the 1870s, the San Francisco cable car system changed the city by giving the public access to some of its hilliest parts, connecting the flatlands at Market Street to the northern wharves and the financial district to the robber-baron mansions on Nob Hill. At one time, there were eight cable car lines in the city, including ones up into Pacific Heights, Russian Hill, and Castro Hill. Today only the Mason-Powell Line, the Powell-Hyde Line, and the California Line remain.

Developed by Andrew Smith Hallidie, the cable car system was designed to be powered from one central point, a nondescript, red-brick building where the loops of cables are centralized. The Powerhouse and Car Barn, as it is known, is still the home of the cable cars and now includes a museum. Within the museum, viewers can see the four cable loops in action, as well as a few of the original cars and other artifacts. *(1201 Mason Street at Washington; 415/474-1887; open daily 9am to 5pm October through March, 9am to 6pm April through September; free admission)*

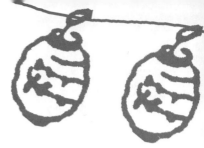

CHINATOWN

OVERVIEW Originally, Chinatown was the area between Kearny and Stockton Streets that runs for about ten blocks from California Street to Broadway. Today, the community includes parts of North Beach as well. Although this segment of the Drive started at the Chinatown Gate, the main section of Chinatown is actually a few blocks to the north. So our real immersion into Chinatown starts on the downhill leg of Clay Street.

Chinatown is the heart of the Chinese community in San Francisco; it also once was the main Chinese population center. Until the middle of the twentieth century, restrictive covenants and other legal restraints on Chinese people kept tens of thousands of new and old residents from China from owning property in or living in San Francisco, except within this area. Forced together, the Chinese residents built businesses and services within the area, maintaining the spirit of a people who kept their cultural identity to become respected and influential members of American communities. Today Chinese and Chinese Americans make up a significant population group throughout the Bay Area.

After the 1906 earthquake, the city hired architects to redevelop the area's buildings, fitting Chinese motifs into structures that met American building codes. This hybrid style, perhaps uniquely San Franciscan, is a key source of interest to tourists. (For more information, visit www.sfchinatown.com.)

Here are some sights both on and off the Drive that will give you a taste of Chinatown life:

• The retail businesses along Grant Avenue are places to linger and shop in Chinatown. You will find simple trinkets for the tourist as well as exceptional pieces of furniture, jewelry, and clothing.

Many of the streets and alleys of Chinatown have been filmed in movies as diverse as Don Siegel and Clint Eastwood's *Dirty Harry* (1972) and Wayne Wang's *Dim Sum* and *The Joy Luck Club*.

- Chinatown is full of stores selling herbs and Chinese medicines. Many of the medicine shops are concentrated around Ross Alley.

- For the most extensive tea collection and a free tasting, visit Ten Ren Tea Shop at 949 Grant Avenue.

- Throughout Chinatown a range of Chinese foods are available. The markets on Stockton and Grant offer inexpensive produce as well as fresh fish (sometimes so fresh they're still alive) and meat. You'll also find shops selling Chinese cooking equipment, such as woks and clay pots. Of course, restaurants abound, spanning many of the tastes and styles of China and the varied budgets of San Franciscans.

- Small lanes and alleys riddle the area. Many of these lanes, where tourists mix with locals and get a feel for daily life in Chinatown, intersect with Grant Avenue. One of the better known is Waverly Place, an alleyway that parallels Grant, just to the east. At 125 Waverly Place is the T'ien Hou Temple, the oldest of the Chinese temples. T'ien Hou, the queen of heaven and sea, protects all transients—tourists, streetwalkers, the homeless, and sailors alike.

- The **Chinese Culture Center** is accessible via the bridge between Portsmouth Square and the Holiday Inn on Kearny Street. It has changing exhibits and performances. (Call 415/986-1822, or visit www.c-c-c.com.)

- The **Chinese Historical Society Museum** opened in 2001 in its new digs—the Julia Morgan–designed **Chinatown YWCA Building** (965 Clay Street)—offering historical displays and information. Check with the society for hours and times (644 Broadway, Suite 402; 415/391-1188, www.chsa.org).

- At 56 Ross Alley, the **Golden Gate Fortune Cookie Factory** offers visitors an opportunity to see how fortune cookies are made, from mixing the batter to forming the folded shape. Special orders are taken for customized fortune slips.

5 **PORTSMOUTH SQUARE** In 1839, San Francisco was called Yerba Buena and was under Mexican control. At that time, Yerba Buena Cove, the shoreline of eastern San Francisco, came inland as far as what is now Montgomery Street. The Mexicans had a surveyor lay out a city square as the welcome point for the port. The main building there was the Customs House.

Captain John Montgomery of the USS *Portsmouth*, with his contingent of US Marines, in 1846 claimed the Mexican Customs House and its surrounding city for the United States. In honor of the "taking" of Yerba Buena by the men of the *Portsmouth*, the park was named Portsmouth Square.

Because the square was situated on the shore of Yerba Buena Cove, it was also the site of the first buildings of the gold rush era. In fact, it was here that San Franciscans were first exposed to the news of gold in the Sierra Nevadas in 1848, when Sam Brannan, a flamboyant newspaper publisher, showed off a bottle filled with gold dust and shouted, "Gold! Gold! Gold from the American River!"

Located between Washington and Clay Streets along Kearny opposite the Chinese Cultural Center (in the Holiday Inn), the square now sits upon one of the few public garages in the Chinatown area.

The upper level has card tables, usually occupied by Chinese men engrossed in a game, as well as a pagoda-topped area. The lower level of the park has a children's playground. Below and behind that is the public parking garage. Also on the lower level is a plaque honoring Andrew Hallidie, the designer of the cable car system. His original route to test the cable cars' viability was on Clay Street from Kearny to Jones Streets, right through the center of Chinatown and along the southern border of Portsmouth Square.

Author Robert Louis Stevenson lived in this area from 1879 to 1880. A monument to him in Portsmouth Square includes a replica of the *Hispaniola*, the fictional ship of *Treasure Island*, along with an inscription from his Christmas sermon.

DIRECTIONS

DRIVING

To continue the Drive from the previous segment (Grant Avenue at Bush): Drive north uphill through the Chinatown Gate two blocks to California Street.

While living at 620 Eddy, Dashiell Hammett rented an apartment at 20 Monroe Street (near Sutter Street) as a place to write without his family around. In 1988, the city of San Francisco officially renamed the one-block street Dashiell Hammett Street.

Turn left (west) onto California; California is extremely steep and has cable cars and tracks running up the center lanes. Drive west on California four blocks to Taylor Street; turn right (north) onto Taylor and continue three blocks to Washington; turn right (east) onto Washington and continue two blocks to Powell Street. Turn right (south) onto Powell, proceed one block to Clay, turn left (east) onto Clay, and take it three blocks to Kearny. Portsmouth Square is on your left. Turn left (north) onto Kearny and drive one block to Washington. (See page 47 for continued driving directions.)

PARKING

In the Union Square area, there are three public parking garages: underneath Union Square, at the corner of Sutter and Stockton Streets, and at O'Farrell and Powell Streets. If you park on the streets at meters, be sure to note the parking signs and tow-away zones. Many streets in the area have specific limitations on parking due to commuter traffic.

In the Chinatown area, parking is even more difficult. Public parking is available at Portsmouth Square (Kearny Street at Clay) and at Saint Mary's Square (Kearny and California).

BUS

Walk two blocks north on Grant Avenue from Bush Street to California Street. Board the California Street cable car, which will take you uphill to Taylor and California Streets. Disembarking there will place you on the top of Nob Hill. From here the walk is level or downhill. Public transportation on the other parts of this segment is a bit less precise. The Chinatown area is served by three buses: the 30–Stockton and 45–Union-Stockton along Stockton and the 15–Third along Kearny. Although none of these routes follows the exact streets of the 49-Mile Scenic Drive, all three go very near it. (See page 48 for continued bus directions.)

A historical plaque on a building at 625 Bush Street (southwest corner of Burritt and Bush) states: "On approximately this spot, Miles Archer, partner of Sam Spade, was done in by Brigid O'Shaughnessy."

WALKING

In this segment, walkers should follow the driving directions.

NORTH BEACH

From Columbus Tower to the Northern Waterfront

N

San Francisco
Bay

JEFFERSON ST

BEACH ST

NORTH POINT ST

BAY ST

THE EMBARCADERO

MASON ST

FRANCISCO ST

CHESTNUT ST

GRANT AVE

LOMBARD ST

COLUMBUS AVE

SANSOME ST

10

11

8

9

GREENWICH ST

FILBERT ST

7

UNION ST

6

NORTH
BEACH

GREEN ST

VALLEJO ST

5

4

BROADWAY

JONES ST

TAYLOR ST

3

PACIFIC AVE

2

1

GOLD ST

HOTALING

MASON ST

POWELL ST

TRENTON

STOCKTON ST

KEARNY ST

MONTGOMERY ST

JACKSON ST

WASHINGTON ST

CLAY ST

SACRAMENTO ST

LEAVENWORTH ST

CALIFORNIA ST

GRANT AVE

PINE ST

BUSH ST

NORTH BEACH

This segment of the Drive covers North Beach, one of San Francisco's most famous neighborhoods. Spend a few hours here, and you'll see why locals and tourists alike flock to the area—its nightlife, street and gallery art, and coffeehouses make this historic area as popular now as it was when it was settled by the original forty-niners.

The dreamy bohemian vibe of the Beat poets in the 1950s and '60s has given way, in much of North Beach, to a slicker, sleeker, more self-conscious scene. But the neighborhood still exudes the Barbary

Coast taste for whiskey and women as well as the European charm of small streets and open-air cafes.

This part of the Drive begins at Columbus Tower, a turn-of-the-century flatiron building converted into Francis Ford Coppola's moviemaking headquarters. It continues up bustling Columbus Avenue past Lawrence Ferlinghetti's City Lights Bookstore to Broadway, where you'll glimpse the more risqué remnants of yesteryear. The Drive catches the quaint end of Grant Avenue, dips down the hill on Lombard for a view of the famous "crookedest street in the world," and then, passing Joe DiMaggio Playground, heads over to Fisherman's Wharf. A small detour will lead you to the neighborhood's oasis at Washington Square or up to the stunning views from Coit Tower.

BEST WAY TO VISIT

North Beach is a great neighborhood to explore on foot, so if you're interested in walking part of the drive, this is an ideal segment. Park your car and enjoy the scenic walk, or, if you're visiting only this segment of the Drive right now, get here by public transportation. Parking in North Beach is difficult. Avoid the frustration and wasted time of looking for a space on the street by parking in the public garage at Portsmouth Square (Kearny at Clay) or in the Vallejo Street Garage (on Vallejo between Powell and Stockton Streets). Then walk through North Beach until you reach Lombard and Mason; a walk or a bus ride up Columbus will return you to your car. On your way to the next segment along the northern waterfront, you can drive the route you have traveled on foot. But not to worry: there's so much to see you'll be happy to have a second chance to soak up the energy of the streets. (See also the Chinatown and Nob Hill segment, which is a great addition to sightseeing in North Beach.)

THE DRIVE

NORTH BEACH OVERVIEW The original settlers in North Beach were the wealthy who had made their money on the sweat of the gold rush miners through shipping, merchandising, banking, and land sales. These were the real winners in the search for gold. But in what was then a small, compact city, the living distance between the elite and the lawless was minimal; therefore, the rich were surrounded by workers and sailors. This was the wild west.

Indeed, there were two beach areas in North Beach, though there isn't even one now. The northern waterfront where the fishermen docked their boats was located on the edge of Bay Street until the bay was filled in to its present location a few blocks north.

Yerba Buena Cove lapped at the very doors of the shops and residences of what is today southern North Beach. Old ships, abandoned by their owners for lack of seaworthiness, were turned into warehouses, houseboats, and other businesses because of the severe building shortage on dry land.

Right along the cove's beaches was a notorious area of saloons, bordellos, and flophouses that became known as the Barbary Coast. That name was bestowed in 1860 by a sailor who was comparing the raucous nature of the neighborhood to the pirate territory by the same name on the coast of North Africa. In San Francisco, vigilante groups patrolled the streets to stop the killings and robberies pervasive throughout this stretch of coastline.

As San Francisco grew, the building shortage eased, and eventually the city sank the ships and docks and filled in the cove. The beach, naturally, was gone, as was the piratelike life along it. The final blow to the Barbary Coast was a small conflagration in 1906 that burned it to the ground. But that's another story.

With the advent of the cable car in the 1870s, the wealthy moved up to Nob Hill, while Italian immigrants joined Latin Americans in

The city of San Francisco has an official walking route called the Barbary Coast Trail, which runs through North Beach and the Financial District to the south, ending at the Ferry Building. That trail is marked on the sidewalk. For further information, check with the Visitors Information Center at Hallidie Plaza, 5th and Market Streets, or check out the book *Walking San Francisco on the Barbary Coast Trail*, by Daniel Bacon.

settling into the North Beach area. After the building of Montgomery Avenue—now called Columbus Avenue—displaced thousands of residents, a decrease in Latin American immigration and an increase in the number of Italians here gave North Beach its lasting identity as the Italian community of San Francisco.

Although Italian residents are now just a small percentage of the population of North Beach, for most of the past 110 years its smells, sights, religion, language, commerce, and neighborhood feel have been reminiscent of Italy. And even today, from the Cathedral of Saints Peter and Paul to Enrico's Restaurant and all of the cafes, bakeries, and delicatessens in between, a European sensibility remains.

A dramatic drop in land and rent values in North Beach in the late 1940s and early 1950s, as residents abandoned the city for the suburbs, led to an influx of artists, musicians, writers, poets, and other cultural intellectuals looking for inexpensive housing. Soon came cafes, nightclubs, and art galleries. This cultural milieu produced the Beat, movement, as the mixture of Bohemian culture and left-wing politics was called. The late *San Francisco Chronicle* columnist Herb Caen coined the term "beatnik" to refer to the young people of the Beat generation, adding the suffix from the Soviet satellite Sputnik because he found both so "far out." Caen meant the name to be condescending, but that meaning was lost as the Beat writers and poets gained recognition throughout the nation. Thus North Beach gained its second lasting identity, one that draws millions of people each year to its streets.

1 COLUMBUS TOWER A thin, three-sided structure rising seven stories above the congested five-way intersection of Columbus and Kearny, the Columbus Tower is distinguished by the green patina of its copper façade and the charming onion-domed cupola that graces its top floor. Work on the building began before the 1906 earthquake and, because it was only slightly damaged, was finished soon thereafter. Once an imposing structure, the Columbus Tower has since been dwarfed by the 48-story Transamerica Pyramid a block or so downhill. In the mid-1970s, film director Francis Ford Coppola bought the Columbus Tower, and since then it has served as the headquarters for his Zoetrope Studios. Other film people, including director Wayne Wang and actor/director Sean Penn, also have offices in the building. On the ground floor is Cafe Niebaum-Coppola, a restaurant and wine bar specializing in products from Coppola's Napa Valley winery. *(916 Kearny at Columbus; Café Neibaum-Coppola, 415/291-1700)*

2 CITY LIGHTS BOOKSTORE AND VESUVIO CAFE One of the keys to the fame of the Beat poets and writers was the establishment and success of their main publisher, City Lights Books. Created by Lawrence Ferlinghetti, a significant Beat poet himself, City Lights published the works of Allen Ginsberg, Diane Ackerman, Gary Snyder, Gregory Corso, Norman Mailer, and others, mostly in paperback and sometimes in pamphlet form.

According to Ferlinghetti, who later became the first Poet Laureate of San Francisco, he opened the City Lights bookstore (261 Columbus Avenue) to help pay the rent for the publishing company. The bookstore became the local outlet for writings by the Beats and other intellectuals. *(415/362-8193; www.citylights.com)*

City Lights and its across-the-alley neighbor Vesuvio Cafe, along with the Hungry i nightclub and the cafes Trieste and Tosca, became the Beat mecca. Of these establishments, only the Hungry i—the "i" stood for "intellectual"—where then unknowns such as Mort Sahl, Woody Allen, Jonathan Winters, the Smothers Brothers, and the Kingston Trio performed, has closed its doors. "I"ronically, a strip club on Broadway now uses its name.

Legend has it that in the mid-1960s, Bob Dylan, Allen Ginsberg, Lawrence Ferlinghetti, Ginsberg's lover Peter Orlovsky, and Orlovsky's brother sat down at **Tosca Cafe** (242 Columbus Avenue). When Orlovsky's brother accidentally walked into the women's rest room, the bartender, not recognizing a single one of the famed artists, threw them all out of the bar.

Jack Kerouac and Dylan Thomas are said to have spent a few drunken nights at Vesuvio Cafe (255 Columbus Avenue). More recently, Van Morrison was asked to smoke his cigar outside of Vesuvio when he violated California's no-smoking law there in 1999. Hanging behind the bar is Paul Kantner's autographed note that reads, "San Francisco—49 Square Miles Surrounded Entirely by Reality." *(415/362-3370; www.vesuvio.com)*

Allen Ginsberg lived in an apartment at 1010 Montgomery (at Broadway) in the 1950s. It was here that he wrote his famous poem "Howl."

On Jack Kerouac Street, on the side of the City Lights building, is a colorful Mexican scene, an adapted design by Tricia Tripp, painted in 1999 by a group of 70 artists. Also of note, the building at 606 Broadway, on the northwest corner of the intersection of Columbus Avenue and Broadway, has a mural showing San Francisco city scenes, created in 1978 by Mirage, Inc.

3 **BROADWAY** Carrying on the "Sin City" tradition of San Francisco's Barbary Coast roots, Broadway between Columbus Avenue and Montgomery Street is the strip of strippers. Despite the thriving sex industry (or perhaps because of it), Broadway is a vibrant street. This is no back-alley red-light district. Sprinkled among the neon lights and scantily clad young women advertising the many topless clubs are restaurants, cafes, and nightclubs where all employees are fully dressed.

The **Condor Club** (300 Columbus Avenue at Broadway) is now just another sports bar, but it's well known for its voluptuous past. Carol Doda danced her way into history here in 1964 when her bare-chested performance made the Condor the first topless bar in the country. Five years later she again inaugurated a trend when she became the first bottomless dancer in the nation. In an opposite twist, the **Hungry i** (546 Broadway) has transformed over the years from offering traditional forms of entertainment at its original Jackson Street location to its current use as a strip club. **Enrico's Sidewalk Cafe** (504 Broadway) has been a San Francisco institution since it opened its doors in 1958. Sit outside and soak up the neighborhood flavor or move inside to enjoy live jazz.

4 **GRANT AVENUE SHOPPING DISTRICT** Grant Avenue is still the main area of commerce in North Beach, but only a few Italian influences remain on this strip. What was once an inexpensive group of shops has changed over the years as upscale businesses such as antique shops and clothing boutiques have moved in. Cafe Trieste (Grant and Vallejo), an original beatnik hangout, and a few sweaty blues bars and pizza joints keep Grant Avenue lively in the Barbary-Beat tradition.

5 **MUSEUM OF NORTH BEACH** Set in the Bay View Bank is a small museum devoted to the North Beach neighborhood. Its photos and memorabilia trace North Beach and Chinatown history of the late nineteenth and early twentieth centuries, with an emphasis on the 1906 earthquake. *(1435 Stockton Street at the corner of Columbus Avenue; open Monday to Thursday 9am to 5pm, Friday 9am to 6pm)*

6 **WASHINGTON SQUARE** If North Beach is the Little Italy of San Francisco, it makes sense that the neighborhood should have the equivalent of an Italian *piazza* at its center. This plaza is Washington Square, the unmistakable grassy trapezoid between Filbert and Union and Stockton and Columbus. It's probably not just a coincidence that the area was designated as a park in 1862, when North Beach was rapidly becoming inhabited by Italian immigrants after many years as a Chilean, Irish, and Mexican quarter.

The office building at 1736 Stockton was designed by famous California architect Bernard Maybeck at the turn of the century.

The oldest building in San Francisco was originally a tent structure at 827 Grant Avenue.

Some thirty years later (in 1897), the statue of Benjamin Franklin was erected in the middle of Washington Square, itself named for the first president of the United States. Dentist Henry Cogswell donated the statue. In 1933, Lillie Hitchcock Coit donated the bronze Volunteer Fireman's Memorial statue on the Columbus Avenue side of the park, in honor of the city's many volunteer firefighters, a group of which she was a very active member. (Read more about Lillie Coit in the Coit Tower section, below.)

After the 1906 earthquake and fire, San Francisco residents camped out in Washington Square while their homes were being repaired. Today, Washington Square still makes its own contribution to San Francisco's blend of many colors and flavors. On any given day at the square, you can see people practicing tai chi in the park, celebrities lunching at **Moose's Restaurant** (1652 Stockton), locals buying focaccia at the **Liguria Bakery** (1700 Stockton), modern bohemians sipping espresso in **Mario's Bohemian Cigar Store Cafe** (566 Columbus), people feeding pigeons or throwing Frisbees, and others filing into the church on the square's northern side.

7 CATHEDRAL OF SAINTS PETER AND PAUL Lawrence Ferlinghetti called this cathedral, at 666 Filbert Street, the "marzipan church," presumably because of its sticky-sweet appearance. The largest church in San Francisco, Saints Peter and Paul was built in 1924 in the neo-Gothic style.

In its early days, the church served the mostly Italian community living in North Beach. Many of the neighborhood residents were fishermen, and it wasn't long before the church became known as the fishermen's church. Living up to this name, the church contains a statue of Santa Maria del Lume, the patron saint of fishermen, and an annual October procession honoring her begins at the church, making its way to Fisherman's Wharf to bless the fishing boats. As North Beach has become more integrated, so has the church; today, mass is held in English, Italian, and Cantonese. (415/421-0809)

8 COIT TOWER AND TELEGRAPH HILL Looming over North Beach is Coit Tower, a gray concrete column atop Telegraph Hill. The tower is a monument to San Francisco's firefighters, built with money donated by one of the city's classic odd-ball heroes: Lillie Hitchcock Coit. When Lillie arrived in San Francisco with her family in 1851, she was only eight years old and already a fire-cracker of a girl. She befriended firefighters, chased fire engines, and even got to douse neighborhood fires herself.

Despite coming of age in the late nineteenth century, Lillie was hardly a demure Victorian lady. She enjoyed gambling, smoking, and wearing pants—not to mention jumping in front of leaping flames. After years of voluntary firefighting, Lillie was made an honorary member of the Knickerbocker Engine Company Number 5.

Against her mother's wishes, she eloped with financier Howard Coit. After he died, she moved to Paris, returning to San Francisco before her death in 1929. She left one-third of her fortune to the city

In addition to outfitting the original Forty-Niners with gold caps on their teeth, dentist Henry Cogswell was an avid prohibitionist during this notoriously bawdy era. His goal—to establish a water fountain for every hundred "watering holes" in the city—was never realized, unfortunately.

in order to erect the tower as a tribute to her favorite civil servants. If Coit Tower resembles the nozzle of a firefighter's hose, it's just a coincidence—the official story is that architect Henry Howard was only trying to construct a monument combining the art deco and classical styles in the small space provided at the summit of Telegraph Hill.

Telegraph Hill itself also has a colorful past. Early Mexican colonists called it *Alta Loma*, meaning "tall ridge." Later settlers named it Goat Hill because of the many goats that lived on its slopes. During the gold rush a semaphore was built on its summit to signal the arrival of ships in the port. A few years later, the West Coast's first Morse code transmitter and receiver were installed in the semaphore. Thus, the hill became known as Signal Hill and eventually as Telegraph Hill. A quick stroll through the neighborhood will show you why Telegraph Hill is one of San Francisco's most desirable neighborhoods—even aside fromt the pristine streets and beautiful homes, the views from atop the hill are some of the best in the city.

Inside Coit Tower is a circular corridor decorated with wonderful Works Progress Administration (WPA) murals depicting life in California through the lens of the social realists. It was the first federally funded mural project for artists

Marilyn Monroe and baseball great Joe DiMaggio took their wedding photos at the Cathedral of Saints Peter and Paul after they were married in San Francisco's City Hall in 1954. (The couple couldn't be married in the Catholic Church because both of them had been divorced.) DiMaggio's funeral service was held here in 1999.

in the United States, providing twenty-five local painters regular work at a salary of $94 per month. After eight months of work on the murals, the doors opened to the public in 1934. You can view the murals for free. A trip to the top of Coit Tower costs $3. *(415/362-0808; open daily 10am to 7:30pm)*

9 **FILBERT STEPS** Although Filbert Street is a public street lined with private residences, it really is a place like none other in the city. Closed to cars and without a road or a sidewalk, the piece of Filbert from Coit Tower down to Sansome is more like a park or a wooded trail than a city street. Alive with birds, flowers, and a canopy of trees, the Filbert Street stairway is one of the most romantic spots in San Francisco. Be sure to check out the charming side streets, Darrell Place and Napier Lane, that jut out north from the steps as you descend past Montgomery to Sansome. At the corner of Montgomery Street and Filbert, you'll see a large white art deco–style apartment building with a bas-relief image of Atlas and the globe. This is where the 1947 Humphrey Bogart classic *Dark Passage* was filmed.

Rather than walking back up the steps, consider crossing Levi's Plaza (1155 Battery Street), world headquarters of the company that makes jeans by the same name, at the bottom of the steps and following the Embarcadero to Mason and Jefferson Streets, where the Northern Waterfront: Fisherman's Wharf segment begins.

10 **VIEW OF LOMBARD STREET** The block of Lombard Street known as "the crookedest street in the world" is best appreciated from the view you'll get as you descend Lombard from Grant Avenue. The zigzag street filled with pink and red flowers will lie clearly before you. Getting to the crooked block of Lombard (between Hyde and Leavenworth) by car involves making several turns, and once you're there you may have a long wait while the traffic in front of you descends. Then again, how often do you get to San Francisco? If you're on foot, walking to the base of the hill is simple, and once there you're welcome to climb the 250 stairs to the top for a breathtaking view of the city.

The slalomlike format of Lombard Street was developed in 1922 when San Franciscans discovered that the 31 percent grade on the hill was too steep for their cars to handle. After World War II, Peter Bercut—then a park commissioner and a gardener—had the hydrangeas planted along each turn of the road. Little known to either tourists or residents is the fact that Lombard is actually in stiff competition with another street just for the ranking of San Francisco's crookedest street. Vermont Street (on Potrero Hill, between McKinley and 22nd Street; see the Mission segment) has seven turns, compared with the eight on Lombard.

11 **JOE DIMAGGIO PLAYGROUND** On your left as you descend Lombard Street and approach Mason is a playground named for the baseball great who as a young boy played ball here with his brothers. Though there's no baseball field here now, local children enjoy the yard, playground, recreation center, and swimming pool at Joe DiMaggio Playground.

DIRECTIONS

DRIVING

To continue the Drive from the previous segment (Kearny Street at Washington): Proceed north on Kearny to Columbus. Turn left onto Columbus (traveling northwest) and then, after a block, turn right (north) onto Grant Avenue. Follow Grant six blocks to Lombard Street. Turn left (west) onto Lombard and continue three blocks to Mason. Turn right (north) onto Mason and follow it six blocks to the waterfront. (See page 63 for continued driving directions.)

PARKING

Parking in North Beach is tight—rarely will you find a spot on the street, though you might do better at the northern end, where Mason heads out to the water. The Vallejo Street Garage (766 Vallejo between Stockton and Powell Streets) is the only public parking garage in North Beach. The neighborhood is mostly flat, except in the area around Coit Tower, so you might be better off leaving your car at one of the parking garages in Chinatown—at Portsmouth Square or Saint Mary's Square—and taking the bus or walking through the southern part of North Beach. Once you've finished there, return to your car and proceed to the waterfront.

BUS

The 15–Third takes you from Portsmouth Square to the southern part of North Beach (get off at Kearny and Columbus), while the 30–Stockton will take you to the waterfront on streets that sometimes parallel the 49-Mile Scenic Drive. (See page 64 for continued bus directions.)

WALKING

In this segment, walkers should follow the driving directions.

NORTHERN WATERFRONT

From Fisherman's Wharf to Aquatic Park

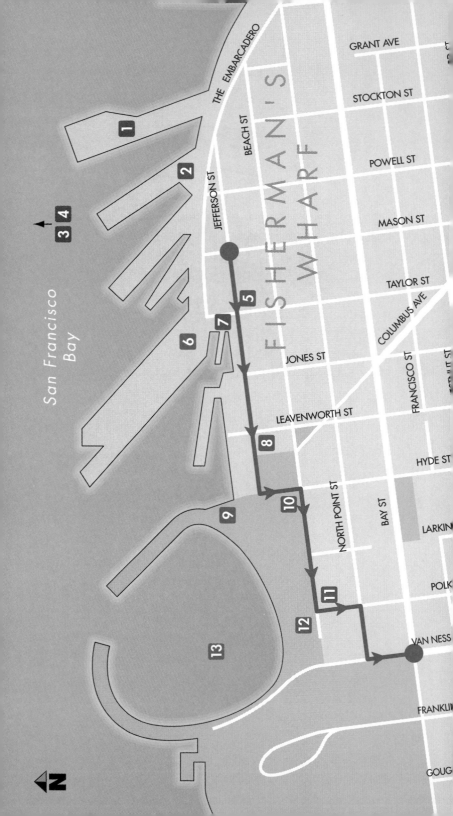

NORTHERN WATERFRONT

Every metropolis has a tourist strip, and San Francisco's happens to be the third most popular in the world. Fisherman's Wharf is *the* quintessential tourist area, bubbling over with everything from candy apples to 3-for-$10 T-shirts. Although you won't see many San Franciscans at the wharf, some only-in-San-Francisco historic treasures remain in the area that will inspire even a jaded local.

Amongst the video arcades, street artists, and trinket shops are hints of the seaside flavor that first made this area famous. On and around Fisherman's Wharf you can eat the best cracked Dungeness crab in town, see an impressive display of historic ships, ogle the adorable California sea lions, and grab a fresh loaf of the classic San Francisco sourdough bread.

Here you can shop at Ghirardelli Square, a former chocolate factory, and the Cannery, a former fish-processing plant, or brush up on local history at the Maritime Museum. From the bar where Irish coffee was first sipped on American shores you can gaze at the cable cars pirouetting at their turnaround.

One of the best ways to appreciate the nautical nature of the wharf is to take a ferry or boat ride from here to Sausalito, Angel Island, or Alcatraz. With the sound of seagulls dancing in the air, the gentle fog brushing your face, and the salty breeze blowing through your hair, you'll understand why people have been rushing through the Golden Gate for a lot more than just a glimpse of gold.

BEST WAY TO VISIT

This is the shortest of the route segments by distance, yet it's jammed with attractions. Depending upon your interests, you could literally spend days here. If you don't have that much time, consider at least visiting the Maritime Museum and the fleet of boats and ships nearby, taking the tour of Angel Island given by the National Park Service, and catching the barking sea lions sunning themselves at Pier 39.

THE DRIVE

FISHERMAN'S WHARF OVERVIEW The number one attraction in San Francisco—and one of the most popular attractions in the world—is the eastern end of the northern waterfront: Fisherman's Wharf. About twelve million people visit this area each year.

The original fisherman's wharf ran along the water's edge when Bay Street, before the building of the northern sea wall and the extension of the landfill, was the northernmost street in San Francisco. The pier where the fishing boats docked extended north into the bay at about Powell. After the land was extended, this area gradually became more industrial. Shipbuilding was the first industry; soon after came a woolen mill and then a chocolate factory, fruit canneries, warehouses, a chemical plant, a smelting plant, railroads to move the cargo to and from the area, and more piers for loading and unloading the industrial raw materials and finished products. Industry extended around the eastern curve of the land as far as Levi's Plaza.

Finally, in 1900, the fishing piers were moved to Taylor Street, the present location of the last such pier that remains. Sightseers began to visit the area in the late nineteenth century, coming to watch the fishermen and to buy fresh fish, bread, and chocolate. For the first fifty years of the twentieth century, the area was alive, thriving on the sea's wealth. Eventually, however, air shipment of fresh fish outmuscled ships and freight trains. Old factories were abandoned for modern structures in more suburban locations.

Starting in the late 1950s, a number of changes occurred that raised this part of the waterfront to its must-visit status, including the opening of the first Cost Plus, now a worldwide retailer, in 1958. With low rents and lots of open parking spaces, the northern waterfront attracted this importer of mostly Japanese home products. Cost Plus filled the warehouses with everything from napkins and candles to dishes, glasses, vases, furniture, and rugs at extremely low prices.

Locals flocked to shop at this extensive and inexpensive store, and in the process they rediscovered the area, which began to change to accommodate their interest. Ten years later, Ghirardelli's old chocolate factory and an old cannery were turned into shopping complexes. The restaurants, trinket shops, and profit-taking "museums" followed as traffic increased along the waterfront. When the pièce de résistance, Pier 39, opened in 1978, along with ferry access to Alcatraz and Angel Islands, the wharf was forever transformed into an extensive (and now expensive) entertainment locale. Gold had finally been struck in San Francisco.

From the wharf it is possible to see San Francisco Bay, from Treasure Island on the eastern curve to Angel Island to the north and over to the Golden Gate, the seaward entrance to San Francisco. The bay has many moods. On a clear day, when there is no fog and the sun sparkles, the sharp lines of the orange Golden Gate Bridge are a dramatic contrast to the green of the shore and the water and the blue and white of the sky. But even in the fog, when bridge, coastal ridge, and bay islands are eclipsed by dense white clouds and the bay's waters turn dark, the vision captivates even the longtime viewer. This is the real San Francisco. *(415/391-2000; www.fishermans wharf.org)*

1 **PIER 39** Make a right turn from Mason onto Jefferson and head away from the Drive to find the main event these days: Pier 39, designed by Walker and Moody and opened in 1978 to be the premier tourist attraction in the city. There are enough things to do here to last an entire day: a carousel, a tunnel-like aquarium, ten restaurants, a protected barrier behind which are an artificial island and hundreds of **sea lions**, and a visitor's center and entertainment area, along with shops of interest to tourists.

The sea lions are protected at this pier because of the 1989 Loma Prieta earthquake. The temblor, 6.9 on the Richter scale, so alarmed and confused these animals that they were herded behind the barrier for their protection. Today, the sea lions have made this pier their home: wooden rafts have been strung together as their out-of-water resting place. It is possible to spend hours watching and listening to these magnificent creatures as they sun themselves. The sea lions feel so secure that they will rest on their platforms just a few yards below where the public stands. They are free to come and go, so the population rises in the summer and declines in the winter, following the regular migratory patterns of these burly animals. Somehow, no matter how far away they might go, they find their ways back to the safety of home. *(north of the Embarcadero at Grant Avenue; 415/705-5500; www.pier39.com)*

2 **PIER 41** Alcatraz and Angel Islands, two historically important islands, are a few miles out in the bay. The Blue and Gold Fleet offers ferry service to both. The San Francisco point of departure for the ferries is at Pier 41. *(north of Jefferson Street and west of Stockton Street; 415/773-1188; www.blueand goldfleet.com)*

These days, the Alcatraz Sharkfest Swim happens twice a year, when hardy swimmers ride a boat out to the island and swim the mile and a half back to Aquatic Park. For information and registration, contact Envirosports, 415/868-1829. For real fanatics, there is the annual Escape from Alcatraz Triathlon, including a 1.5-mile swim from the island as well as an 18-mile bike ride and an 8-mile run.

3 **ALCATRAZ ISLAND** Alcatraz was the home of a federal penitentiary for decades. Famed criminals such as Al Capone and "Machine Gun" Kelly spent many years here. Movies starring Edward G. Robinson, George Raft, James Cagney, Burt Lancaster, Clint Eastwood, and Sean Connery continue to glorify its Elba-like past.

But the island's history also includes the conflict between the white settlers and the original Native Americans. In 1969, a group of Native Americans seized the by-then-deserted island, claiming it as theirs. Support for the siege was widespread but spotty; for instance, the members of the musical group Creedence Clearwater Revival donated a boat to the group on the island so they could fish.

The Native Americans held the island for about two years before the federal government raided and retook the land and the former prison. In 1972, it was incorporated into the Golden Gate National Recreation Area (GGNRA).

Today, the National Park Service has developed a tour of the grounds and buildings. On some days, guest speakers on the "Rock" include former guards of the prison, and even a reformed—but still rugged—former inmate.

Movies filmed here include *Escape from Alcatraz* (1979), *Murder in the First* (1995), *Birdman of Alcatraz* (1962), *The Rock* (1996), *Point Blank* (1967), and *The Enforcer* (1976).

Alcatraz was considered impossible to escape from because it was thought that no one could swim across San Francisco Bay. But that didn't stop prisoners from trying and, perhaps, succeeding. No prisoner is known to have made it across to the San Francisco shores, but those declared missing might have swum the distance. *(www.nps.gov/Alcatraz)*

4 ANGEL ISLAND Angel Island's history involves another chapter in American life: immigration. From 1910 to 1940, the federal government used Angel Island as a detention and immigration point for immigrants, primarily Chinese, entering the United States, similar to Ellis Island in New York's harbor. California's history is filled with racism toward the Chinese, Japanese, and Filipino immigrants and their descendants. Yet commerce demanded cheap labor, and so Asians were allowed in to meet this need. Quotas on Asian immigration restricted their number, while entry for Europeans was more open. Getting in often depended upon whom the Asian immigrant knew—a relative or friend or an association that would sponsor the applicant. After the State of California codified this practice, some immigrants created documents to show they were married to or related to someone already in the United States in order to qualify for admittance. These people became known as "paper wives" and "paper relatives" because their relationships existed only on paper. For many in the late nineteenth century, Angel Island was the last stop in their journey, where officials decided whether to turn them back or permit them to enter—a decision often based primarily on their race and/or national origin.

The island was used as a detention center, military hospital, and quarantine facility. During World War II, it was a Japanese internment camp. After the war, the military abandoned it, and it was left unused for about thirty years.

When Angel Island was added to the GGNRA in 1972, the National Park Service developed an information center and opened the island to visitors. Although most of the furnishings of the deten-

During the height of tourist season, this area has more than 3,000 pedestrians per hour, making it one of the busiest streets in San Francisco.

tion barracks are gone, the poems and other writings on the walls remain for us to read and remember what it meant to come to America.

The island is a great place to hike, with a five-mile perimeter trail and the 781-foot Mount Livermore. Bicycles are available for rent, or you can take a tram tour. For the historically minded, docents will guide you through the Immigration Station and other sites on the island on weekends only. Campsites are reasonably priced for peak and off-peak seasons. Bring what you need on the ferry from Pier 41 or from Tiburon, even the charcoal for your barbecue. There is only a cafe on the island. *(415/705-5555; www.angelisland.org)*

5 **JEFFERSON STREET ENTERTAINMENT ZONE** A walk along Jefferson Street between Powell and Jones Streets is reminiscent of walking the Atlantic City or Coney Island boardwalk—without the boards. The northern side of the street, along the water, is lined with major attractions and restaurants, while the southern side offers traditional entertainment fare, from video arcades to the Ripley's Believe It or Not! Museum. Inexpensive T-shirts, souvenirs of almost every imaginable shape and size, fast-food shops, and an assortment of street performers vie for visitors' attention.

The south side of Jefferson Street explodes with energy. Among the internationally known features are the Wax Museum (145 Jefferson; 800/439-4305; www.waxmuseum.com; open weekdays from 9am to 11pm and weekends from 9am to midnight) and Ripley's Believe It or Not! (175 Jefferson; 415/771-6188; www.ripleysf.com; open Sunday through Thursday 10am to 10pm, Friday and Saturday 10am to midnight). Plenty of fast-food and T-shirt and souvenir shops to see here, too!

6 **PIER 45** To see the few remaining fishermen in northern San Francisco at work, visit Pier 45 early in the morning. The last vestiges of the industry that was a mainstay during the late nineteenth century and most of the twentieth century, today's tiny fishing fleet still brings in a sizable catch—about 20 million pounds each year. Parts of the historical fishing fleet, made up of the old Italian *felucche* and the newer Monterey clipper fishing vessels, can be found near Shed B at the pier and along Jefferson as far west as Hyde Street.

On the eastern side of the pier is the permanent berth for the USS *Pampanito* and the visiting dock for active U.S. Navy vessels. The *Pampanito*, a submarine built at the naval shipyards in Portsmouth Harbor, New Hampshire, sank five Japanese warships during World War II. *(415/775-1943; www.maritime.org; open Sunday through Thursday 9am to 6pm, Friday and Saturday 9am to 8pm)*

In summer, the National Liberty Ship USS *Jeremiah O'Brien* offers another tour of interest. It docks here from May to October (the rest of the year you'll find the ship at the Embarcadero; see the Eastern Waterfront segment) and gives visitors a chance to see the only functioning liberty ship left from the D-Day armada. Launched in 1943, this merchant marine vessel took only 56 days to build. On certain weekends (check the calendar on their web site), the *Jeremiah O'Brien* has "steaming weekends," when the oil-fired engines and the coal-fired stoves are lighted. The ship also has cruises twice a year—in late May for Memorial Day weekend and in early October during Fleet Week. *(Pier 45, May to October; 415/441-3101; www.ssjeremiahobrien.com; open daily 9am to 3pm except major holidays)*

7 **FISH ALLEY AND TAYLOR WHARF** Although the south side of Jefferson has some fast food, none compares with the walkaway Dungeness crab cocktails available across the street. Patterned on the traditional chowder walkaways prepared for turn-of-the-century fishermen, this quick seafood lunch was created by Tomaso Castagnola in 1916. The Castagnolas were among the many Italian fishing families who moved from running fishing boats to running fresh-fish restaurants in the last century, along with the Aliotos, the Scomas, and the Sabellas.

These family-owned restaurants are located primarily along Jefferson east of Taylor Street, a stretch known as Fish Alley. Most serve until midnight, and they validate parking. If you are looking for a meal that is a San Francisco tradition, try the *cioppino*, an Italian tomato-based stew made with a variety of shellfish and seafood. It is to San Francisco what *bouillabaisse* is to Marseilles and gumbo is to New Orleans.

A walk down an alley to Scoma's (Pier 47; 415/771-4383) will bring you to the restaurant's fish-receiving building, upon which hangs a mosaic of San Francisco scenes. Created by John O'Shanna, the mosaic pays homage to the artistic style of Benny Bufano, the famed sculptor, long-time regular customer at the restaurant, and friend of Al Scoma.

Isidore Boudin, founder of the Boudin Bakeries located throughout the city, invented San Francisco's signature taste: the sourdough French bread sold along the wharf. Boudin came up with this crusty, tangy bread in 1849 when he couldn't find the ingredients he normally baked with at home in France. When he substituted yogurt for commercial yeast, the sourdough was born. The bread you buy at Boudin Bakery today is a direct descendant of the original recipe: a bit of "mother dough" from the previous day's batch is added to each day's lot. The healthful bacteria contained in the dough give the bread its special zing.

8 **THE CANNERY** In the Cannery, a shopping complex inside a building that once housed the largest peach cannery in the world, only the four exterior walls date back to the original structure. The inside was gutted and replaced with a separate building-in-a-building in 1968. The red-brick walls of the old building, constructed in 1907 for the California Fruit Canners Association, were left for the look. The Chart House on the bottom floors is decorated with some of the antiques collected by newspaper tycoon William Randolph Hearst. *(2801 Leavenworth, south of Jefferson Street; 415/771-3112; www.the cannery.com)*

The storage space for the old cannery is known as the Haslett Warehouse (Hyde south of Jefferson). Now owned by the Maritime Museum, it was originally built in three stages between 1907 and 1909.

9 **HYDE STREET PIER** At the foot of Hyde Street, visitors get a glimpse of the vessels that made maritime activity so prominent in San Francisco's early years. The Hyde Street Pier is part of the San Francisco Maritime National Historical Park that also includes Aquatic Park, the USS *Pampanito* (Pier 45), and the Maritime Museum.

The six historic ships berthed at the Hyde Street Pier were instrumental in developing the Pacific Coast. The *Balclutha*—considered the park's prize exhibit—was built in Scotland in 1886. She sailed many times from Europe, traveling around Cape Horn to San Francisco, before being stationed here in the early 1930s as an entertainment venue. This beautifully restored merchant ship illustrates the life of nineteenth-century seamen with displays of nautical equipment, living quarters, and the ship's mechanics.

The *Eureka* was built in 1890 and soon became the largest passenger ferry of its time, carrying commuters from across the Bay to work in San Francisco. Today the *Eureka* is the largest floating wood vessel in the world.

The tugboat *Hercules* dates from 1907. She towed sailing ships out to sea and log rafts to lumber mills. The scow schooner *Alma* made her first voyage in 1891 and carried bulk cargoes such as lumber and hay around the Bay Area until highways and bridges became ubiquitous. Her flat bottom was perfect for navigating the shallow waters of the bay.

The *Eppleton Hall*, a paddle-tug built in England in 1914, is much like the boats that towed ships into San Francisco during the gold rush years. The *C. A. Thayer*—built in 1895—was an important factor in the rapid growth of California cities in the early twentieth century. She is one of two surviving schooners from the fleet of 900 that carried lumber from the Northwest to the burgeoning townships in California. *(415/556-3002; www. maritime.org; open daily 9:30am to 5:30pm)*

10 POWELL-HYDE CABLE CAR TURNAROUND

The end of the line for the Powell-Hyde cable car is at its turnaround northeast of the intersection of Hyde and Beach Streets, offering a quick and easy way to get from downtown to the western end of Fisherman's Wharf. Riders disembark at Victorian Park, between the Cannery and Ghirardelli Square. Crowds also form around the turnaround to embark.

11 GHIRARDELLI SQUARE

Not everyone who came to California during the gold rush struck it rich right away. Domenico Ghirardelli, an Italian living in Peru in the mid-nineteenth century, arrived in California in 1849 and headed immediately for the Sierras in search of gold. Fortunately for us, he was one of the unlucky gold-diggers. Ghirardelli soon moved to San Francisco to cultivate a different sort of riches: chocolate.

Ghirardelli owned a few shops near Portsmouth and Jackson Squares, but he ran into problems, including arson and then bankruptcy. He turned the business over to his sons, and in 1893 they moved the chocolate operation to the space we now know as Ghirardelli Square. The building they bought had previously been the Pioneer Woolen Mill—an operation that had made wool blankets and uniforms for the Union Army during the Civil War.

The Ghirardellis operated their chocolate factory at this location until the early 1960s, adding more buildings as the business grew. When they moved their manufacturing plant to a bigger space in the East Bay, the brick buildings on the waterfront were converted into the shopping center now known as Ghirardelli Square. It was the first project in the United States to convert historic industrial buildings into a tourist attraction.

In addition to its many shops and restaurants, Ghirardelli Square offers visitors a glimpse of its Willy Wonka past. On the ground floor of the Clock Tower building is the Ghirardelli

While waiting for the cable car at Victorian Park, designed by landscape architect Thomas Church, some people slip into the Buena Vista Cafe across the street to sip an Irish coffee. Local legend has it that the first Irish coffee on American shores was poured here in 1952.

Chocolate Manufactory. There you can see the roasters, mills, and mixers of yesteryear while indulging in all kinds of sweet temptations. *(900 North Point Street; 415/771-4903; www.ghirardelli.com)*

12 MARITIME MUSEUM

One look at the Maritime Museum and you'll immediately understand how it got its name. The art deco building looks like a 1930s-era ocean liner and houses a collection of nautical treasures. But the building, erected as part of the Aquatic Park WPA project, was not designed to be a museum. The ground floor was originally a public bathhouse and center for water sports, while the upper floor was a lounge and restaurant. During World War II, Army offices were housed in the waterfront building. It became the Maritime Museum in 1951.

The museum is filled with treats for the history buff, architectural connoisseur, nautical aficionado, and art lover alike. The mural by artist Hilaire Hiler in the main room is an underwater fantasy, a departure from the typical WPA style of social realism, which depicted life as it was for the common people of that era. At the museum's entrance is a green slate intaglio carved by Sargent Johnson, Northern California's only African American WPA artist.

Upstairs, history lovers will enjoy the gold rush–era panoramic pictures of San Francisco. Other rooms on this level exhibit remains from nineteenth-century ships, relics from the whaling industry, and models tracing the development of steam technology. On the third floor, visitors learn about nautical methods of communication, with hands-on exhibits on Morse code, lighting, and radio systems.

The **Red and White Fleet** runs bay and ocean cruises from Pier 43 ½ (415/673-2900; www.redandwhitefleet.com). It also runs a ferry to Richmond, in Alameda County (510/464-1030).

If all this isn't enough to make you want to stop and visit, here are two more incentives. First, with its large windows that stretch across the entire waterfront side of the building, the museum offers some of the best wind-free vistas in San Francisco. Second, entry to the museum is free. *(Beach Street at the foot of Polk Street; 415/556-3002; www.maritime.org; open daily 10am to 5pm)*

13

AQUATIC PARK Bridging the tourist bustle of Fisherman's Wharf and the cultural and natural serenity of Fort Mason is Aquatic Park. This picturesque cove offers all kinds of recreation: the city's only bayfront beach; a paved promenade for jogging, walking, or biking; and swimming clubs such as the Dolphin Club for the truly brave.

In 1866, Frederick Law Olmsted, the designer of Central Park in New York City, suggested that the cove now known as Aquatic Park be transformed from industrial use to recreational use. It wasn't until some seventy years later that his idea came to fruition. Aquatic Park was established in 1935 when Roosevelt's WPA devoted the funds necessary to convert what had been a dumping ground for rubble from the 1906 earthquake into a recreational facility. If you have the time for a little pedestrian exploration, walk the curved Municipal Pier to its tip for a fabulous bridge-to-bridge panoramic view of San Francisco Bay.

At the foot of the Municipal Pier is a paved path heading west from Van Ness Avenue. This path (discussed in the Best Way to Visit section of the Northern Waterfront: Fort Mason segment) also has magnificent views of the Marin Headlands.

DIRECTIONS

DRIVING

To continue the Drive from the previous segment (Mason Street at Jefferson): Turn left (west) onto Jefferson Street. Follow Jefferson four blocks to Hyde Street. Turn left (south) onto Hyde and follow it one block to Beach Street. Turn right (west) onto Beach Street and continue two blocks to Polk Street. Turn left (south) onto Polk and proceed one block to North Point Street. Turn right (west) onto North Point and drive one block to Van Ness Avenue. Turn left (south) on Van Ness to Bay Street and turn right (west). (See page 74 for continued driving directions.)

PARKING

Parking is extensive but expensive around Fisherman's Wharf. The priciest lots are near Pier 39, just off the Drive but an important attraction. Metered parking spots line the streets close to Fisherman's Wharf. Two blocks south (south of Bay Street), there is limited two-hour street parking without meters. Parking at the western end of the Wharf south and west of Ghirardelli Square is moderately priced and sometimes free.

Ferries to and from Sausalito, Tiburon, Marine World in Vallejo, Muir Woods, and the Napa-Sonoma wine country come to and depart from Pier 41. Call the Blue and Gold Fleet (415/773-1188; www.blueandgold fleet.com).

BUS

During the daytime, the 32–Embarcadero runs along Jefferson Street from Mason Street to Hyde and Beach Streets at Aquatic Park. Walk west along Beach to Ghirardelli Square and the Maritime Museum; turn left (south) on Polk and follow it to Bay. Turn right (west) on Bay and follow it to Van Ness Avenue. The 42–Downtown Loop (both Gold Arrow and Red Arrow) runs on North Point, two blocks south of the Wharf area, day and evening. (See page 74 for continued bus directions.)

WALKING

In this segment, walkers should follow the driving directions.

NORTHERN
WATERFRONT

From Fort Mason to the Presidio Gate

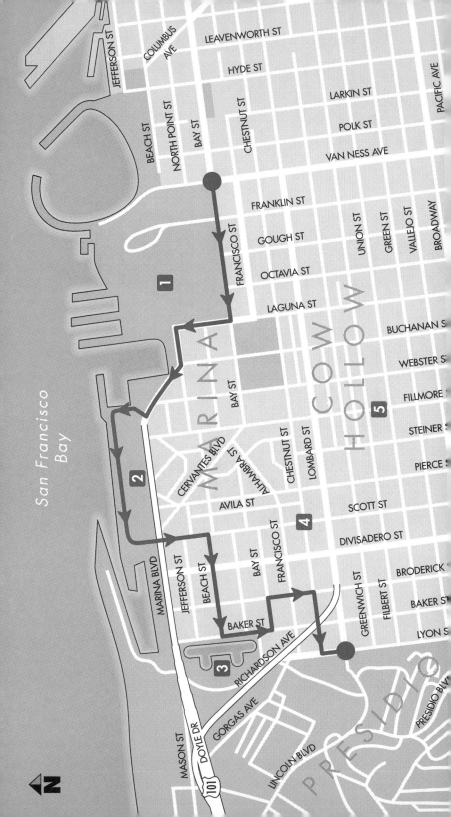

NORTHERN WATERFRONT

On this segment of the Drive, you'll see the part of the waterfront that San Franciscans really use and enjoy. At the Golden Gate National Recreation Areas of Fort Mason and the Marina Green, locals fly kites, stroll beside the bay, or linger at their yacht clubs. With a very different feel from the tourist-centered Fisherman's Wharf, this area is designed more for recreation than for consumption. Whether you fancy visiting the small ethnic and craft museums at Fort Mason, getting some exercise on the parcourse at the Marina Green, or feeding the ducks at the Palace of Fine Arts, this segment of the Drive is both scenic and fun. Its flat and bright route includes some of San Francisco's most creative institutions, such as the legendary vegetarian restaurant Greens and the hands-on science and technology museum the Exploratorium, and it conveys the real reasons San Franciscans love their waterside town.

BEST WAY TO VISIT

Be aware of traffic moving quickly along Bay Street and Marina Boulevard. Try to get a look at the mural on the eastern side of the Safeway store on Laguna. The turnoff on Marina Boulevard into the Marina Green parking lot is followed almost instantly by another left. This is a great place to stop (parking is ample and free) and stretch your legs or take in a view of the Golden Gate Bridge. Committed walkers may want to try the Golden Gate Promenade. It begins where Van Ness Avenue meets the Municipal Pier at Aquatic Park (at the end of the Northern Waterfront: Fisherman's Wharf segment) and continues along the waterfront to Fort Point near the foot of the Golden Gate Bridge, about 3.5 miles. The Promenade offers magnificent views of the San Francisco Bay, including Angel and Alcatraz Islands, the Golden Gate Bridge, and the Marin Headlands.

The route makes a few seemingly unnecessary turns after passing the Palace of Fine Arts. Stick with them, though, because they'll guide you along the easiest route to the Presidio gate.

THE DRIVE

GOLDEN GATE NATIONAL RECREATION AREA OVERVIEW

The Golden Gate National Recreation Area (GGNRA) is a collection of 360 scattered open spaces, both large and small, in Marin County, San Francisco, and San Mateo County. The GGNRA was created because of the determination of one man, the late Philip Burton, long-time San Francisco assemblyman and congressman. It was designed to save what was still unspoiled and to return to recreational use areas that were no longer needed to defend San Francisco Bay.

The GGNRA has come of age with the decision to return the Presidio, a former military base, to civilian use. Although administration of Fort Mason and the Presidio is in the hands of specific trusts with congressional oversight, the National Park Service has primary responsibility for most of the sites that make up the GGNRA. Parklands include Mount Tamalpais National Park, the Marin Headlands, and Muir Woods in Marin County; and the Maritime National Park, Fort Mason Center, Crissy Field, Fort Point, the Presidio, Baker Beach, Land's End, Sutro Heights, the Cliff House, Ocean Beach, and Fort Funston in San Francisco.

The 49-Mile Scenic Drive passes by and through many of the San Francisco parts of the GGNRA. In the Northern Waterfront: Fisherman's Wharf segment, the route took you past the Maritime Museum and Hyde Street Pier and offered information about Angel and Alcatraz Islands. In the next two segments (the Presidio and Sea Cliff to the Sea), you will visit most of the rest of San Francisco's part of the GGNRA. In this segment, the route centers on Fort Mason and the Marina Green.

1 FORT MASON AND THE GREAT MEADOW Named for the military governor of California, Colonel Richard Mason, who in 1850 was ordered by President Millard Fillmore to establish this fort, the post became a national park in 1972 and became part of the GGNRA when the recreation area was established. Congress maintains control of the site through its creation of the Fort Mason Trust.

The buildings at Fort Mason date back as far as 1855, when the Officers' Club, on the eastern side of the GGNRA administrative buildings, and other structures in the compound were built. Accessible from Bay Street at Franklin (the eastern entrance to Fort Mason), this area was overrun by squatters in the 1850s and early 1860s. They were cleared out during the Civil War to make room for armament batteries. Today, besides the GGNRA administration, this part of the fort also houses an international hostel.

The broad space between the east buildings and the west buildings is called the Great Meadow. With its magnificent view of the Golden Gate and Marin County, it is a gathering place for thousands, fog or no fog, who come to view the July Fourth fireworks displays.

At the western end of the fort (Laguna and Beach Streets) is the Fort Mason Center. Dozens of nonprofit groups and theatrical troupes, a noted vegetarian restaurant, and a few small museums and galleries reside here. Sandwich boards placed at the entrance to the center list the schedule of daily events. Pick up a copy of *Fort Mason Center*, a monthly guide to activities. *(415/979-3010; www.fortmason.org)*

The following are some of Fort Mason Center's residents of note:

• Playhouses and theatrical companies: Bay Area Theatresports performs improvisational theater all year round, including an annual festival (Building B; 415/474-8935; www.improv.org). Chinese Cultural Productions promotes Chinese dance and music (Building C; 415/474-4829; www.ccpsf.org). Internationally recognized Magic Theatre presents plays by known and unknown American playwrights (Building D; 415/441-8822; www.MagicTheatre.org). The Young Performers Theatre is a professional children's theater presenting a number of plays each year (Building C; 415/346-5550; www.ypt.org).

• Music: The Blue Bear School of American Music has day and evening programs in all types of "American" forms (Building D; 415/673-3600; www.bluebearmusic.org).

• Museums: There are several small museums at the center. All charge admission, but on the first Wednesday of every month admission is free. The Mexican Museum presents exhibits on the art and culture of Mexico and the Americas (Building D; 415/202-9700; www.mexicanmuseum.org; open Wednesday to Sunday 11am to 5pm). Museo ItaloAmericano has two galleries and a research library on Italian and Italian-American art and culture (Building C; 415/673-2200; www.museoitalianoamericano.org; open Wednesday to Sunday noon to 5pm). Next door is the San Francisco African American Historical and Cultural Society, with a gallery featuring exhibits on African and African American art and culture (Building C; 415/441-0640; open Wednesday through Sunday noon to 5pm). The

San Francisco Craft and Folk Art Museum has exhibits and educational programs on contemporary crafts and the history of folk art (Building A; 415/775-0990; www.mocfa.org; open Tuesday through Friday and Sunday 11am to 5pm, Saturday 10am to 5pm).

- Art: The Coffee Gallery presents the works of students and faculty of the City College of San Francisco Fort Mason Art Campus. Both the gallery and the school are housed in Building B (415/561-1840; www.ccsf.org).

- Radio: Radio Bilingue, a distributor of Spanish-language news and programming, broadcasts the show *Linea Abierta* every weekday from Building D (415/674-0925; www.radiobilingue.org).

- Food: One of the country's most famous vegetarian restaurants, Greens Restaurant, along with its Greens-to-Go takeout service, can be found serving lunch, dinner, and Sunday brunch (Building A; 415/771-6222; Greens-to-Go: 415/771-6330). Cooks and Company meets the needs of both carnivores and omnivores visiting Fort Mason Center (Building B; 415/673-4137).

2 **MARINA GREEN AND THE YACHT HARBOR** In front of the Yacht Harbor is another expanse of lawn known as the Marina Green. Locals and tourists alike come here to fly kites, picnic, and, on the weekends, watch San Francisco's "armada" of sailing vessels catch the breeze on the waves of the bay. Both the San Francisco Yacht Club and the Saint Francis Yacht Club just a little farther west are private. On a clear day, the displays of natural and human-made forms, from Angel Island and the Marin County coastline to the Golden Gate Bridge, are breathtaking.

3 **PALACE OF FINE ARTS AND THE EXPLORATORIUM** The Beaux-Arts building known as the Palace of Fine Arts is one of the few structures remaining from the Panama-Pacific International Exposition held in San Francisco in 1915. Bernard Maybeck

A spin-off of the Exploratorium—the first one ever—opened in Paris in 1999 as the Explor@dome. The Exploratorium hopes to open other partnership museums throughout the world in the coming years.

designed the rotunda and its colonnade to look like Roman ruins. Unlike the rest of the Exposition buildings, which were demolished when the event was over, the Palace of Fine Arts has become a permanent fixture in the San Francisco landscape. In the 1960s its plaster was replaced with concrete, and the building has been standing strong ever since. Nowadays, residents flock to the water's edge to feed the ducks, go for a walk, or sit in the sun—and you should too. The scenic backdrop of the Palace of Fine Arts is a favorite spot for picture-taking, so you may see a wedding party in full dress during your visit. *(Baker Street at North Point)*

Inside the Palace of Fine Arts is the Exploratorium, a hands-on museum devoted to science and technology. It was founded by physicist and educator Frank Oppenheimer, brother of physicist J. Robert Oppenheimer (who helped develop the first atomic bomb), and opened in 1969. As much a laboratory of learning as a source of amusement, the Exploratorium is a favorite field trip for almost every kid who grew up in San Francisco.

Fortunately, adults also enjoy many of the exhibits. Dance your way through the Shadow Box to see your shadow frozen on the screen behind you. Tease your senses on the table of pins and needles. Those with strong stomachs won't want to miss the cow's-eye dissection. If you're planning ahead or have lots of time in San Francisco, reserve an afternoon in the Tactile Dome with a group of friends. This mind-boggling sensory adventure is a preferred activity for birthday parties for city kids and their kids-at-heart adult friends. *(3601 Lyon Street at Richardson Avenue; 415/561-0360 for a recorded message; 415/561-0362 to make a reservation for the Tactile Dome; summer hours daily 10am to 6pm, Wednesday until 9pm; winter hours Tuesday through Sunday 10am to 5pm, Wednesday until 9pm; admission fee, except on the first Wednesday of the month, when it is free)*

4 **MARINA DISTRICT AND CHEST-NUT STREET** Once a sleepy residential neighborhood with many elderly residents, the Marina District has become a trendy area inhabited mostly by young professionals. The Marina—built on a combination of drained wetlands and bay landfill—was the San Francisco neighborhood most affected by the 1989 earthquake. Locals say that after the quake did its damage, many of the Marina's elderly sold their homes and moved to more solid ground. With its easy access to waterside recreation and short bus ride to the Financial District, the Marina quickly became a choice location for San Francisco yuppies when the housing market opened up.

Baseball great Joe DiMaggio lived in the Marina District on and off for fifty years with his parents, siblings, and wife Marilyn Monroe. He bought the house at 2150 Beach Street for his parents at a cost of $14,600 when he signed with the Yankees in 1937. When Joe died in 1999, the house sold for $1.1 million.

A stroll down Chestnut Street, the Marina's merchant strip, reveals the old-meets-new nature of the neighborhood—it feels, by turns, like a glitzy cosmopolitan hub or the main street of a small village. You'll see sleek young men and women sipping lattes at Peet's Coffee while doing business on their cell phones and, across the street, other neighborhood residents ordering from the butcher whom they call by his first name.

5 **COW HOLLOW AND UNION STREET** Cow Hollow refers to the area on the northern slope of Pacific Heights, south of the flatlands of the Marina. The neighborhood got its name in the 1870s because of the many dairy farms there at that time. Like the Marina District and Pacific Heights, Cow Hollow has become an affluent area. The spine of Cow Hollow is Union Street, lined with designer boutiques and trendy restaurants. On Friday and Saturday nights the bars around Union, Fillmore, and Chestnut form a virtual frat row, brimming over with post-collegiate types engaging in the traditional sports of beer drinking and mate seeking.

DIRECTIONS

DRIVING

To continue the Drive from the previous segment (Bay Street at Van Ness): Follow Bay Street four blocks to Laguna; turn right (north) onto Laguna and left (west) two blocks later onto Beach Street. Bear right onto Marina Boulevard. Turn right (north) into the Marina Green parking area, curve around through the area, and turn left (south) at the small craft harbor entrance. Coming out of the parking area, continue straight ahead (south) on Scott Street two blocks to Beach Street. Turn right (west) onto Beach and follow it to its end (three blocks) at Baker Street. Turn left (south) onto Baker Street and drive two blocks to Bay Street; turn left (east) onto Bay, drive one block, and then turn right (south) onto Broderick. Turn right (west) onto Chestnut and cross the large boulevard called Richardson to reach Lyon (two blocks). Turn left (south) onto Lyon and drive one block to Lombard Street, to the entrance to the Presidio. (See page 88 for continued driving directions.)

PARKING

There is plenty of parking on most of this segment, except in Cow Hollow and the Marina District. Along the Drive itself, find free two- to four-hour parking (depending upon the area) at the administrative offices area of Fort Mason (entering from Franklin and Bay Streets), at the Fort Mason Center (entering from Laguna and Marina Boulevard), and along the Marina Green (the Drive actually includes this parking area). The folks at City Hall are considering metering the green's parking areas, so check the signs. For the Exploratorium at the Palace of Fine Arts, free street parking is sparse but is backed up by free parking on the northwest side of the palace near Crissy Field. Within Cow Hollow and the Marina District, two-hour unmetered and one-hour metered parking is available.

BUS

No bus routes follow the 49-Mile Scenic Drive in this area. Here is what you can do: Take the 30–Stockton to the corner of Bay Street and Van Ness Avenue to see Fort Mason. Make sure to get a transfer from the bus driver when you pay. You are permitted two boardings within one-and-a-half hours.

If you want to go to Fort Mason Center, take the 30–Stockton to Laguna Street and walk four blocks to the entrance, or transfer to the 28–19th Avenue, which goes directly into the center, where the museums and galleries are. When you are ready to go on, retrace your steps and reboard the 30–Stockton, which continues on to Chestnut Street in the Marina District. A short walk west to Lyon and south to the Presidio gate completes this segment. (See page 88 for continued bus directions.)

WALKING

From Bay Street at Van Ness, walk west along Bay Street one block to the first Fort Mason entrance gate at Franklin. Enter the fort to visit the administration area. Return to Bay Street and continue west three blocks to Laguna. Turn right (north) onto Laguna and proceed two blocks to Beach Street. Follow Beach one block to Fort Mason Center entrance. Turn right (north) to enter Fort Mason Center.

(*Note:* There is a prettier walk that starts at the foot of Van Ness Avenue near the Municipal Pier. Follow the left fork, which heads west behind the administrative buildings on a cliff along the water. This paved trail has views of the Golden Gate Bridge and Angel and Alcatraz Islands and brings the walker to Fort Mason Center. The walk continues along the esplanade of the waterfront, eventually taking the walker to Fort Point, about 3.5 miles from its start.)

After visiting Fort Mason Center, return to Beach, which, by turning right, puts you on Marina Boulevard. Turn right (north) and follow the signs into the parking lot of the Marina Green. Walk along the waterfront alongside the parking area. At the end of the lot, turn left (south) and continue out onto Scott Street. Follow Scott two blocks and turn right (west) onto Beach. Follow it to its end (three blocks) at Baker Street. Turn left (south) onto Baker, walk five blocks to Lombard Street, and turn right (west). Continue one block on Lombard to the entrance to the Presidio at Lyon.

THE PRESIDIO

From the Presidio Gate to El Camino del Mar

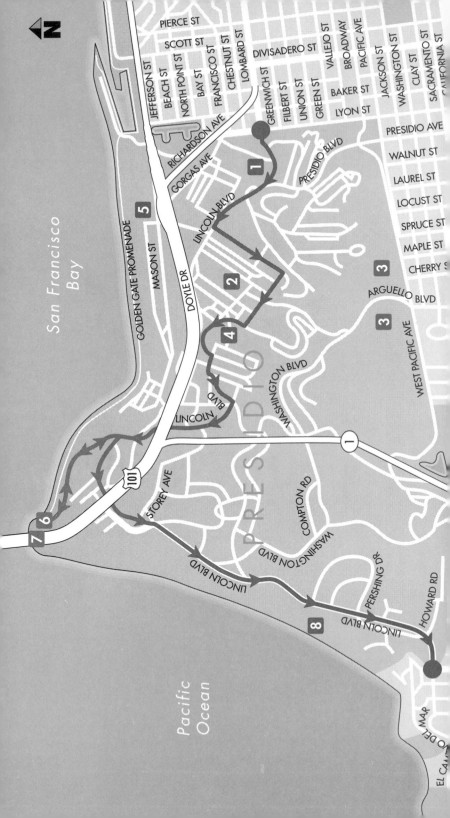

THE PRESIDIO

The Presidio is a beautiful work in progress. Its 1,480 acres of cypress and eucalyptus forest, rugged coastline, and colonial architecture are being converted from a U.S. Army base into a financially independent national park.

In many ways, the Presidio has always been a work in progress. From its historic roots as a Spanish military post, to its stint under Mexican reign, to its heyday as a prestigious military base, the natural landscape here on the edge of the Golden Gate has been shaped by a variety of cultural influences in the last 300 years. All the while, the Presidio has maintained an environment that highlights its pastoral and wooded beauty as well as its beachfront splendor. As you follow the Drive through the Presidio, you'll pass the Letterman Complex, the site-to-be of George Lucas's digital studios; the Main Post, former military parade grounds; Fort Point, the dramatic base of the Golden Gate Bridge; and sweeping vistas of the Pacific Ocean along Baker Beach. The natural and varied landscape makes the Presidio an excellent place for outdoor recreation. For hiking, swimming, surfing, fishing, golfing, bowling, jogging, biking, or just a breathtaking view, no urban park in the world compares to the Presidio.

BEST WAY TO VISIT

Whether you decide to explore the Presidio on foot or by car, we recommend that you begin your trip with a stop at the visitor's center (see Main Post, below). From here you can decide whether you want to leave your car parked at the Main Post and traipse through the many natural trails in the Presidio or drive to sights further west. At the visitor's center you can get maps, learn about the land, and find out about special programs.

THE DRIVE

THE PRESIDIO OVERVIEW When José Joaquín Moraga established a *presidio*, or military post, at the southern entrance to San Francisco Bay in 1776, the land was flat and sandy, with strong winds coming in off the ocean, and there virtually were no trees. He chose the site because it was the best position from which to defend the bay's opening gate.

The Presidio was part of an overall plan by the Spanish government in Madrid to maintain its claim over the lands of California against the Russian and British presence in the late eighteenth century. The irony, of course, was that, although neither Russia nor Britain succeeded in taking down the Spanish government, the Spanish settlers and their offspring did just that forty-five years later and established the nation of Mexico.

The Mexican government's focus on overland invaders from the United States and the continued conflict over the Russian and British presence below California's northern border caused the garrison to be moved to Sonoma, about fifty miles north, leaving the Presidio abandoned. In 1847, the New York Volunteers took the outpost in the Mexican War, establishing an American military presence there.

The Presidio was abandoned again at the end of the war, and it wasn't until President Millard Fillmore in 1850 established vast military-controlled tracts for defense (later scaled back to today's Fort Mason and Presidio boundaries) that the military began its return. After the building of Fort Point, a seven-year project finished in 1862, a main post was laid out in the area of the original Spanish outpost, and for the next 140 years the Army maintained a major presence in the life of San Francisco.

The Presidio's building plan continued onward, including the officers' quarters on the east side of the parade grounds and barracks on the west side. Troops fighting in the Indian Wars of the 1860s and 1870s moved in. Soon the area was opened for public use.

In 1883, the Army Corps of Engineers, headed by Major W. A. Jones, began a massive forestation plan, planting more than 100,000 pines, eucalyptuses, and cypresses to create a great woods. Later, skirting the woods, a nine-hole golf course (later expanded to eighteen holes) was built, and more trees were planted throughout the course. The trees anchored the sandy dunes into hills of green, and the park was transformed into its present magnificent form.

Other areas of the Presidio were also built, including the enlisted men's quarters (now known as the Baker Beach Apartments), a public health hospital, a military hospital (later torn down and replaced by the Letterman Complex, which is also planned for demolition soon), the batteries along the coast, Crissy Field, San Francisco's first airport, and Fort Scott, a now-abandoned post separate from the main post yet on the grounds of the Presidio.

In 1994, during the decision-making process on base closures, the federal government designated the Presidio for civilian use with a small military presence. The lands were administratively split between the National Park Service and the Presidio Trust and were placed into the Golden Gate National Recreation Area. Today, the primary focus of the trust is to determine how to make the Presidio a self-sustaining area and how the more than 500 historic buildings will be used or removed. The trust's mandate from Congress lasts until 2013. At the present time, its strategy is to develop an office park and private residences within the Presidio, and to use the rental income to maintain the park. San Francisco residents and visitors alike enjoy the beautiful park and the views of San Francisco Bay.

1 **LETTERMAN COMPLEX** The Letterman Complex, on your right just after you enter the Presidio, is in a state of rapid change. Since the nineteenth century, the site has been a hospital and research facility for the military. In 1999, however, the Presidio Trust sought developers for the site as part of the plan to support the Presidio as a national park. Because the Presidio must be financially self-sufficient by 2013, leasing the Letterman site is an extremely important part of this process. George Lucas has entered into a ground lease that gives him the right to develop the land and is planning to move his digital studios, now in Marin County, here. In addition to building a new 23-acre facility with offices for his Industrial Light & Magic, THX Group, Lucas Arts Entertainment Co., Lucas Online, Lucas Learning companies, and a new Visual Effects Archive and Advanced Digital Training Institute, Lucas has proposed a "great lawn" as part of the 14 acres committed for public use. In interviews, Lucas has said that he hopes to turn the Presidio into a "Lincoln Center of the west for the digital film arts."

2 **MAIN POST** When the Presidio was an Army base, the Main Post was the administrative heart of it all. Clustered here were housing, a hospital, a social club, and the military parade grounds. You'll approach the Main Post as you turn left on Funston from Lincoln. The first building on your right is the Old Station Hospital. Built in 1857, this is the oldest structure in the Presidio that is still standing in its original form. Formerly a military museum, the building is now used for administrative offices. Behind it (accessible only by foot) are two restored cottages from the time when the Presidio was used as a shelter for those whose homes were destroyed in the 1906 earthquake.

The row of houses farther up on Funston is known as Officers' Row because officers and their families lived there when the Presidio was a U.S. Army base. Built in 1862, these are the oldest homes in the Presidio. Now they are leased to private individuals.

On Moraga Avenue, the Officers' Club is on the left—a sprawling Spanish-style building with two cannons at the entrance. Formerly known as the Commandante's Quarters, this is the site of the first building in San Francisco, originally erected in 1776. The Spanish and Mexicans used this space as quarters and headquarters; the American army used it as its officers' club. Today, only the foundation of the original building remains.

Further down Moraga, at number 385, is the Herbst International Exhibition Hall. Its rotating displays can be educational or artistic. There is usually a small admission fee; inquire at the hall or at the visitor's center for information about current exhibits.

If you turn right on Montgomery, you enter the original parade grounds of the Main Post—now a vast stretch of parking lot. Continue down Montgomery and stop at the National Park Service Visitor's Center in Building 102. It is a fascinating place, with information about trails and recreation in the Presidio as well as displays on the history and geography of the land. Look for brochures on special programs, or ask the employees about guided walks, concerts, and cannon demonstrations, some of the many organized activities in the park (415/561-4323; www.nps.gov/prsf). The brick buildings along the west-

Animal lovers can catch a glimpse of the Park Service's horses at the stables that formerly housed the Army's cavalry. Nearby is the quirky Pet Cemetery, resting place for Princey, Smoochy, and Polka, among many other military cats and dogs buried here. Overgrown weeds and tilting headstones add to the charm of this cemetery. Although it is officially closed to new interments, locals continue to bury their dear departed in the picket-fenced plot, nestled at the base of a support to Doyle Drive (McDowell Avenue off Lincoln Boulevard).

ern end of the parade grounds (where the visitor's center is located) are nineteenth-century barracks, now converted to administrative use.

On the eastern end of the parade grounds is Building 39. Once a barracks for World War II infantrymen and, later, the Sixth U.S. Army headquarters, the building is now home to the San Francisco Film Centre. An association of twenty-one film-related organizations, the Film Centre includes sound editors, post-production houses, special-effects companies, and the San Francisco Film Society, which runs the San Francisco International Film Festival. *(39 Mesa Street, Suite 110, The Presidio; 415/561-5000; www.sfiff.org)*

3 RECREATION IN THE PRESIDIO
The Presidio is a playground for adults and children alike. Here are a few of the activities and sights that it provides for the public. Inquire at the visitor's center for more detailed information and maps.

Hikers and bikers may be interested in exploring the **Bay Area Ridge Trail**, a 400-mile trail that circumnavigates the entire San Francisco Bay, passing through 2½ miles of the Presidio.

For children, the Presidio has two wonderful playgrounds: **Mountain Lake Park** and **Julius Kahn Playground**. Both have large climbing structures, slides, and swings. Julius Kahn also has a baseball field, and Mountain Lake Park features a lovely pond with swans and ducks.

Those interested in military history may want to visit **Fort Scott** and the many military batteries that line the coastal areas of the Presidio. For organized recreation, the Presidio has a bowling alley and a golf course, both open to the public.

4 **NATIONAL CEMETERY** The military began burying its dead in 1884 in the 10 acres just west of the Main Post. This was the first designated national cemetery on the West Coast. The area has grown to its present 28-acre size. It is now closed to new burials; those eligible for military burial are now interred in Colma, south of San Francisco.

The headstones mark the resting places of men and women who died in every war since the Civil War. Serene and magnificent, the cemetery is surrounded by the forest and looks out over the bay.

Although the National Cemetery is officially closed to new burials, the rules were bent to inter Philip and Sala Burton, husband and wife and representatives to Congress who fought for the creation of the Golden Gate National Recreation Area and the inclusion of the Presidio within it.

5 **CRISSY FIELD** Until the late 1990s, Crissy Field was a large tarmac area, used primarily as a parking lot for waterfront events and the place to party when watching fireworks on July Fourth. But as part of the plan to convert the Presidio into a national park, the Park Service is transforming the former Army airfield into a tidal wetland, its natural habitat.

This $27 million restoration project is one of the Park Service's biggest undertakings in improving an outdoor space. In restoring the original landscape and biodiversity of this land, the Park Service has created dunes, marshland, mud flats, and a lagoon and dike, and has planted 20,000 seedlings and slips of native grasses and shrubs. All this has attracted sixty species of birds, including dowitchers, sandpipers, herons, and terns, as well as the fish and invertebrates they thrive on. Eventually, the shoreline park will include a community environmental center, a shoreline promenade, and a grassy meadow.

6 **FORT POINT** President Fillmore's orders in 1850 to establish a military reservation meant that a fortification was needed to protect against an ocean invasion. So most of the budget for the Presidio went into the nine-year construction of Fort Point, at the Golden Gate. Started in 1853 and finished in 1862, the French-style brick-and-mortar hexagon and its seawall were to be the sentry point. Although the fort was used, it eventually became clear that there were few threats from the west. As the Indian Wars spread, the Army focused inland, and the fort was no longer needed.

Today, the Fort is a museum. The building is open without charge and includes some artifacts of life in the military during the 1800s. Walkways with iron railings overlook the main courtyard, with windowed rooms set back toward the walls. There are no doors between the rooms, and the visual effect is startling, almost dizzying, when you look down the corridor. The National Park Service has brought electricity only into those areas that need it, so the visitor gets the feeling of the dark life as well as the drafty design of the building.

On the second floor are two photographic exhibits: "Women in the Military" and "African-Americans in the Military." The photos chronicle the vital role of women who risked their lives in nonmilitary capacities on the front lines, as well as the troops of the Ninth Cavalry, an all-black unit that played an important role in the Spanish-American War and in protecting the president of the United States while he was in San Francisco.

The seawall, while protecting the fort against the strong currents and waves of the ocean and bay, also acts as a great vista on San Francisco. The lure of those high waves brings surfers out for a daring ride along the rocky shore. Torpedo Wharf, just east of Fort Point, is a fishing pier open to the public. And the Golden Gate Bridge soars above the fort itself, making Fort Point feel more like Fort Pint, a tiny building next to the might of modern construction. *(415/556-1693; www.nps.gov/fopo/ index.htm)*

7 GOLDEN GATE BRIDGE In the real estate world, the slogan is "Location, location, location." And one of the most dazzling locations in the world is the San Francisco Bay's opening to the Pacific Ocean, called the Golden Gate. Spanning the gate, enhancing its dazzle and just as mighty, is the Golden Gate Bridge. The mix of beautiful setting and architectural style makes this bridge one of most impressive human-made structures in the world.

Built in less than four years and privately financed during the Depression, the bridge was initially the vision of Joseph P. Strauss, chief engineer of the construction and prime mover of the project from its inception. The bridge structure was redesigned from Strauss's original concept by Irving F. Morrow, incorporating important structural and artistic changes. His moving of the crossbeams from the tops of the bridge posts to below the driving deck, and his inclusion of the art deco–style arches and tele-

Janet Leigh leaped into the bay from Fort Point in Hitchcock's masterpiece *Vertigo*.

scoping structures have created a sense of soaring as one travels north-bound; the bridge's graceful curve of suspension wires frames the city's skyline as one travels south. Whether seen in clear skies or partially covered by the drifting fog, the bridge contrasts with and enhances its natural environment.

The Golden Gate, as a name associated with the entrance to the bay, was coined by Captain John C. Frémont in 1848. The color of the bridge is not gold but officially "international orange," tending toward a reddish-brown tone. Opened in 1937, a year after the San Francisco–Oakland Bay Bridge to the East Bay, the Golden Gate Bridge radically altered the transportation plan of the Bay Area, moving away from water travel to cars, buses, and commuter trains.

At both ends of the Golden Gate Bridge are turnout vistas from which you can walk across the bridge. Two-hour metered parking allows the walker plenty of time to traverse the 4,200-foot span, which on an ordinary day is about a one-hour round-trip stroll. The winds sweep in off the ocean, so it gets blustery and cold out there. Bicyclists and walkers share the eastern walkway during the week, with the bicyclists moving to the western side of the bridge on weekends.

On the San Francisco side of the bridge are a visitor's center and store, cafe, and gardens. A memorial honoring the eleven workers who died building the bridge, a marker for its sister bridge in Japan—the Seto Ohashi Bridge—and a statue of Strauss are among the scattered objets d'art in the area. When at cliffside, look down for a bird's-eye view of Fort Point. The visitor's area in Marin has spectacular views of the San Francisco skyline.

8 **BAKER BEACH** Baker Beach forms the southwestern border of the Presidio. A right turn off Lincoln onto Bowley will lead you down to the beach. The fenced-in building next to the parking lot is a water treatment plant. (The Presidio uses its own water source, separate from the city's.) Baker is a popular beach with San Franciscans. Set in a parklike cove and equipped with picnic tables and a large parking lot, it is the first beach to fill up on a hot day in the city. The far north end of the beach is clothing-optional. At Battery Chamberlain, just behind Baker Beach, a demonstration cannon shooting takes place the first weekend of every month. Check with the National Park Service Visitor's Center for schedules. *(415/561-4323; www.nps.gov/prsf/pphtml/facilities.html)*

DIRECTIONS

DRIVING

To continue the Drive from the previous segment (Bay Street at Van Ness): Turn right (west) from Lyon onto Lombard and drive through the Presidio entrance gate. The road curves right (northwest) and, after two blocks, joins Presidio Boulevard; it then veers right (north by northwest) and becomes Lincoln Boulevard.

Turn left (south) onto Funston and follow it two blocks to Moraga. Turn right (west) onto Moraga and follow it five blocks to Infantry Terrace. Bear right (north) and go three blocks to merge with Lincoln Boulevard again. Stay left on Lincoln. With the exception of turnoffs for the National Cemetery, Fort Point, Golden Gate Bridge, and Baker Beach, stay on Lincoln until it exits the Presidio, becoming El Camino del Mar. (See page 97 for continued driving directions.)

PARKING

There is plenty of free parking throughout the Presidio, but less is available at Fort Point.

BUS

The 28–19th Avenue, the 29–Sunset, and the 43–Masonic all run through the Presidio. (See page 98 for continued bus directions.)

WALKING

From the Presidio entrance at Lombard and Lyon, walkers should follow the driving directions, or hike the trails with guidance from the National Park Service Visitor's Center (Building 102, Main Post; 415/561-4323; www. nps.gov/prsf/ pphtml/facilities.html).

SEA CLIFF TO THE SEA

From 25th Avenue to the Cliff House

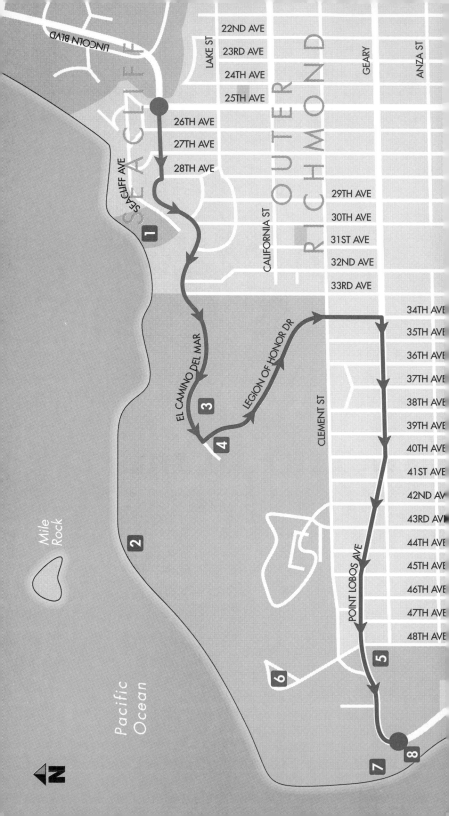

SEA CLIFF TO THE SEA

Travel west on the Drive through Sea Cliff—the Bel-Air of San Francisco—to see some exquisite seaside mansions. Then head into Lincoln Park, a coastal treasure with walking trails along the ocean's cliffs, a public golf course, and a fine-arts museum at the California Palace of the Legion of Honor. After leaving the park, the Drive takes you west through the outer part of the Richmond District, a culturally diverse residential neighborhood. When you reach the cliffs at the end of Geary, visit Fort Miley, a tribute to the USS *San Francisco*'s importance in World War II, or explore the Rome-like ruins of the historic Sutro Baths. This segment ends at the Cliff House, a nineteenth-century landmark overlooking Seal Rock and the sparkling Pacific Ocean.

BEST WAY TO VISIT

This segment of the Drive is easy, and the parking is good. Consider parking at Fort Miley for a walk around the bluffs at Land's End, listening to an organ performance at the museum on the weekend, stopping at the Cliff House overlooking the ocean for hot chocolate if you're driving (or a cocktail if you're not), picnicking in Sutro Heights Park, or swimming at China Beach. This area is known for its dense fog, though the vistas are stunning with or without sun.

THE DRIVE

SEA CLIFF OVERVIEW The luxurious neighborhood known as Sea Cliff is nestled on the rugged coast between the Presidio and Lincoln Park. Hanging over China Beach, Sea Cliff was developed in the early 1900s with large houses built in the Mediterranean style. Exclusive and pristine, Sea Cliff is now home to many of San Francisco's most famous movie stars. Robin Williams—known around town for hosting fun-filled Halloween parties for the kids in his neighborhood each year—lives on Sea Cliff Avenue, in the mauve house flying a flag with a blue wolf.

1 **CHINA BEACH** Named for the Chinese fishing camp that was located here at the end of the nineteenth century, China Beach is a hidden treasure, favored by locals in the know. This calm little cove below Sea Cliff features a sandy beach, picnic tables, clean bathrooms, and a pier, as well as lifeguards during the summer months. Follow Sea Cliff Avenue until it dead-ends at a parking lot across the street from the Swiss Consulate (a large beige house flying the red-and-white Swiss flag). Walk down to the beach from here.

2 **LAND'S END** Nature trails for hiking or biking along the cliffs above the Pacific offer great views of Marin and the Golden Gate Bridge. They are accessible from both Lincoln Park and Fort Miley. You will see signs for Land's End as you enter Lincoln Park. You can also reach the trails from the north side of the Merrie Street parking lot near Fort Miley. Below this area were many shipwrecks, victims of the strong waves and fog of the Golden Gate.

Pulitzer Prize–winning newspaper columnist Herb Caen—loved by San Franciscans for his astute observations of city life—wrote this in 1996: "It was one beautiful Tuesday—not a cloud in the sky, no fog on the horizon. I drove through Sea Cliff, a highly regarded faubourg which never struck me as Very San Francisco. With the sun beating down on its palms, lawns, and well-kept houses, it was, as usual, Pasadena meets Santa Barbara."

3 **LINCOLN PARK** As you head out of Sea Cliff and into Lincoln Park, you'll pass a sign that says "Land's End." This refers to the federally owned trail along the coast, though the park you'll drive through is the city's Lincoln Park. The entire Golden Gate National Recreation Area boasts impressive coastal views and walks along its scenic bluffs. But only at Lincoln Park can you soak in the scenery while playing golf or visiting a world-class fine-arts museum.

The Lincoln Park Municipal Golf Course is a public course just down the hill (toward Clement Street) from the Palace of the Legion of Honor. The eighteen-hole course was originally a municipal graveyard, mostly for immigrants—which explains the Chinese tombstones at the first and fifteenth holes. *(34th Avenue and Clement Street; 415/750-4653)*

4 CALIFORNIA PALACE OF THE LEGION OF HONOR

The California Palace of the Legion of Honor is a three-quarter-scale copy of the original *Palais de la Légion d'Honneur*, originally built in 1786 in Paris under Napoleon's reign. Alma Spreckels, a San Francisco aristocrat of French descent, commissioned the museum in the early 1920s to promote the appreciation of French art in California. The collection has now expanded to include works from all of Europe, among them paintings by Titian, Rubens, El Greco, Rembrandt, Poussin, Monet, and Degas as well as more than a hundred sculptures by Rodin. The museum scenes in Hitchcock's *Vertigo* (1958) were filmed here in Gallery 6.

The museum's 1924 Skinner organ, made of mahogany, ebony, and ivory, with 4,526 pipes literally built into the walls of the building, was rebuilt in the 1990s and now is capable of full symphonic range. In the gallery, the upper walls are made of canvas to allow the sound to be released into the dome of the room. The museum's front entrance has a frieze that opens to allow the music into the courtyard. Concerts are held on Saturday and Sunday each week at 4pm and are included with admission. The museum's entrance fee allows same-day entrance to the M. H. de Young Museum in Golden Gate Park. *(415/750-3624; museum hotline: 415/863-3330; open Tuesday to Sunday 10am to 5pm, first Saturday of the month until 8:45pm; free on the second Wednesday of the month)*

OUTER RICHMOND OVERVIEW

The Outer Richmond is the western half of the Richmond District, which spans from Golden Gate Park on the south and from Arguello Street on the east to the ocean on the west. Once known as the Great Sand Waste—the area was made up of miles of rolling sand dunes until Golden Gate Park was developed in the late nineteenth century—the Richmond is now home to a vibrant multiethnic community of mostly Russians and Asians. Frugal food lovers will love this foggy residential neighborhood, where excellent inexpensive restaurants whose owners are of Slavic, Asian, and Irish descent are sprinkled along the merchant streets of Geary, Clement, and California.

5 **SUTRO HEIGHTS PARK** Overlooking the Cliff House on the eastern side of Point Lobos Avenue, Sutro Heights Park commands a mighty view of the coast heading south. It was once the home of Adolph Sutro, owner of the Sutro Baths, who bought the property and designed a house and extraordinary landscaping. Just as was done in the Presidio, Sutro forested the land to hold the sandy soil and create his lawn. He also built a parapet so he could view his good fortune.

Sutro's house is gone, but some of the garden's statuary remains. A quiet, underused neighborhood park, this is a great place to view the Pacific coastline, read, or have a picnic (weather permitting).

6 **FORT MILEY AND USS *SAN FRANCISCO* MEMORIAL** Fort Miley was a 54-acre piece of land east of Point Lobos owned by the U.S. Army, of which 29.5 acres are now the site of the Veterans Administration Medical Center in San Francisco. It was originally purchased from private sources in 1893 to bolster the defense of the Golden Gate, and its gun battery was finished in 1897. It was known as the Reservation at Point Lobos and was considered a subpost of the Presidio.

In 1930, San Francisco was chosen as the site for a veterans' hospital. Although application for construction on the Presidio was denied by the War Department, at the request of the Federal Board of Hospitalization Congress allocated money to purchase 25 acres, and later an additional 4.5 acres were acquired. The hospital, built in 1934 in a California-Spanish-Mayan style, is a complex of about two dozen buildings and is accessed from Clement Street at 42nd Avenue.

The rest of the original acres are now part of the Golden Gate National Recreation Area. Mostly wooded, it lies between the USS *San Francisco* Memorial and Land's End. There is a Ropes Adventure Course here, run by the Recreation and Leisure Studies Department of San Francisco State University. Contact 415/338-6883 or www.fortmileyropes.org for additional information.

The USS *San Francisco*, a heavy cruiser stationed in the Pacific theater of World War II, guided a convoy of ships to Guadalcanal to support the American invasion of that island. During the night of November 12 to 13,

1942, the *San Francisco* led a group of American ships into battle with fourteen Japanese ships that were heading toward Guadalcanal.

The *San Francisco* suffered severe damage while engaging the lead Japanese battleship. Even so, the battleship was crippled and the Japanese convoy was stopped, allowing the Americans to defeat the Japanese troops who arrived the following day.

The memorial commemorates the USS *San Francisco*'s importance in that battle. Two pieces of the ship's bridge form a V around a flagpole and plaque. The memorial overlooks the Pacific Ocean, where the ship once roamed, and has views of the Marin Headlands across the Golden Gate entrance to the San Francisco Bay, as if always on a vigil to protect the city for which it was named.

7 SUTRO BATHS From the Merrie Street parking lot, the Sutro Baths lie open for your inspection. Although they may look like ancient ruins, the archaeological dig probably won't begin for many centuries.

Situated just north of the Cliff House, these ruins are all that are left of a bawdier time in San Francisco toward the end of the nineteenth century. The three-acre site was built by Adolph Sutro in 1886 and featured a complex of six pools in a glass dome with an accompanying arcade that included restaurants, art galleries, an amphitheater, and a museum.

Business was brisk at the turn of the century but fell off significantly by the time of the Depression. Closed in 1964, the bath house burned to the ground as it was being demolished in 1966. The site is now part of the Golden Gate National Recreation Area.

8 CLIFF HOUSE In addition to the Sutro Baths, Adolph Sutro also owned the Cliff House, which at the turn of the century was in its third incarnation as a seven-story hotel. Sutro, known as the "king of the Comstocks" for building an important tunnel in Nevada during the Comstock silver mine's great years, went on to become mayor of San Francisco. At one point, he owned one-twelfth of the land in the city.

The Cliff House was originally built in 1858 and was rebuilt in 1864, 1896, and 1909. The building now standing was remodeled in 1950. The multilevel structure includes a visitor's center, views of nearby Seal Rocks—and, on a clear day, of the distant Farallon Islands—and restaurants. On its lower level is the Musée Mechanique, a gallery filled with antique arcade machines that still work, reminders of what once was here. On the deck outside the Musée Mechanique is a small building, the Camera Obscura, containing a camera with a pivoting lens. The subject stands inside a room, and the lens rotates, including the subject in a panoramic shot projected onto a screen. *(1090 Point Lobos Avenue; 415/386-3330; GGNRA Cliff House Visitor's Center: 415/556-8642)*

DIRECTIONS

DRIVING

To continue the Drive from the previous segment (the Presidio exit at El Camino del Mar): Continue west on El Camino del Mar, through Sea Cliff, and follow it into Lincoln Park (the first sign says "Land's End Recreation Area"). Turn left (south) and go past the Palace of the Legion of Honor on the right. Continue south to exit the park on 34th Avenue, and continue one block to Geary. Turn right (west) onto Geary; bear right to join Point Lobos Avenue at 42nd Avenue. Follow Point Lobos Avenue as it curves to the Cliff House. (See page 111 for continued driving directions.)

PARKING

In Sea Cliff, two-hour street parking is available. The areas approaching and within Lincoln Park around the Palace of the Legion of Honor and along the trails on the north end are also free. At Fort Miley, there is a large parking lot at the USS *San Francisco* Memorial (off El Camino del Mar).

At the Sutro Baths and the Cliff House is a large parking lot that you can enter at Merrie Street and Point Lobos Avenue as you descend from El Camino del Mar. Another parking lot is across the street, at the foot of the hill leading to Sutro Heights Park. Street parking is available in front of the Cliff House but is often crowded and difficult to maneuver into. One way or another, you will probably have to walk the hill a bit.

BUS

The 29–Sunset, which travels on Lincoln Boulevard through the Presidio, will take you to 25th Avenue and El Camino Del Mar, just where the bus exits the Presidio. Get off there to see Sea Cliff.

There is no direct bus service between Sea Cliff and Lincoln Park. You have two choices: Make your way on foot to the Palace of the Legion of Honor in Lincoln Park, where you can board the 18–46th Avenue to reach the Cliff House area. Or, if you wish, return to 25th Avenue and El Camino del Mar, take the 29–Sunset to Geary, and transfer to the 38–Geary heading west to the Cliff House–Sutro Baths area, missing the Lincoln Park section of the route. (See page 111 for continued bus directions.)

WALKING

In this segment, walkers should follow the driving directions.

OCEAN BEACH & THE SUNSET DISTRICT

From the Great Highway to Sunset Boulevard

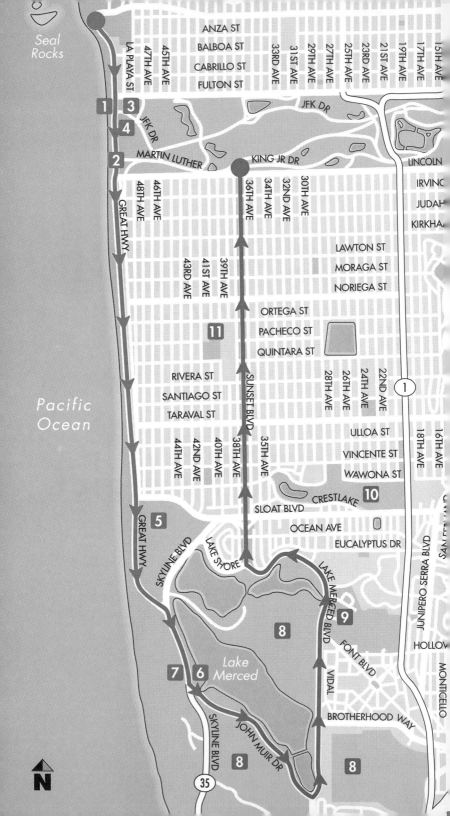

OCEAN BEACH & THE SUNSET DISTRICT

This segment of the Drive covers the city's western frontier, where modest prewar homes line the wide oceanside streets and the residents are proud to live in one of the last city neighborhoods where parking is not a problem. This is the area that was once so far out that San Franciscans of the late nineteenth century called it the Outlands.

Although the Sunset is known for its dense fog, sleepy residential blocks, and time-warped merchant strips, the area is nonetheless ripe with its own kind of excitement. Large expanses of land and the raging Pacific Ocean have made the Sunset a bastion of recreation, with several golf courses and soccer fields as well as beaches for surfing and hang gliding. The Drive takes you on the Great Highway along the stretch of coast known as Ocean Beach, passing the historic windmills in Golden Gate Park and the visitor's center and restaurant at Beach Chalet. It swings past the gun club and the boathouse at Lake Merced, where you can hear the lions roaring from the nearby zoo. Skirting the western edge of the San Francisco State University campus, the Drive heads toward Golden Gate Park on Sunset Boulevard. A short detour will lead you to Stern Grove, a eucalyptus-rich park, or Fort Funston, the seaside cliffs where hang gliders take flight. This part of the Drive covers important territory often overlooked by Barbary Coast–focused tourists and eastern-oriented city residents.

BEST WAY TO VISIT

Even San Franciscans admit that the weather plays an important part in the city's charm. This is especially apparent along the coastline. Fog movement wraps the western part of the city as Christo wrapped the Reichstag, creating a temporary visual change in the environment that makes us aware of nature's palette. Northern California's ocean breezes can be cold, even when the sun is shining—and when the fog moves in, it becomes even colder.

A couple of fine ways to enjoy this part of the Drive: on a sunny day, pack a lunch and picnic on the decks of Fort Funston while watching the magic hang gliders overhead. Or arrive at dusk to watch the sunset (if it's not covered by fog) from the Beach Chalet's restaurant.

Because this is a long segment along the park and beach, we recommend that you drive, allowing time to stop and check out the sparkling sights along the way. This is a good walk for nature lovers, but those hungry for urban treasures would probably rather whiz by in their cars. If you are walking the entire way, be prepared to spend a full day on your feet.

THE DRIVE

1 **OCEAN BEACH** Ocean Beach, a 6-mile stretch of sand and sea, reaches south beyond Fort Funston to the San Mateo County border. Although it's a popular destination for wet suit–wearing surfers, the National Park Service advises against swimming or surfing at Ocean Beach. There are no lifeguards here, and the strong undertow and brisk waters can be dangerous. For swimming you're better off at Baker Beach in the Presidio or China Beach in Sea Cliff. On a hot day—however infrequent these may be—Ocean Beach fills to the brim with sunbathers.

San Francisco recognized early on that the coastline should be protected from encroachment and tenaciously fought its development. It is hard to imagine that, because of the beach's inaccessibility to the common folks of San Francisco (only a few could afford the carriages necessary to reach the ocean), thousands of people lived their whole lives in the city without ever seeing the Pacific.

As the beach heads southward, it becomes less hospitable to the sunbather and of more interest to the environmentalist. Grasses and shrubs grow in the sandy areas in a more-or-less open ecology. *(along the Great Highway from Balboa Street to the San Francisco border with San Mateo County; GGNRA Cliff House Visitor Center: 415/556-8642)*

2 **GREAT HIGHWAY** The unpaved road carved out in the 1860s through the sands between the Cliff House and what became Sloat Boulevard was designated the Great Highway in 1874. The drifting sands were finally controlled by the embankments and retaining walls built in the 1930s by the Works Progress Administration (WPA). Today it is a four-lane expressway, a back-door route that connects with Skyline Boulevard, which heads south to the peninsula and the Highway

Rock star Chris Isaak lives in the Sunset District, within walking distance of Ocean Beach. He is a regular rider on these rough waves. He has described surfing at Ocean Beach as "like some kind of German Expressionist film—all foggy, cold, and dark, and nobody around. Just me and the sharks."

Few remember the Playland amusement park that once thrived on the flats between Golden Gate Park and Sutro Heights, where a Safeway supermarket now stands. Playland wasn't the original business on this site, however. It replaced the Golden Gate Ostrich Farm, an important source of feathers and skins for fashions of earlier times.

The carousel of the defunct Playland is now thrilling riders at Yerba Buena Gardens.

1 coastal route to Monterey Bay. *(from Balboa Street to Skyline Boulevard)*

3 **WINDMILLS AND TULIP GARDEN** The two windmills at the west end of Golden Gate Park, visible on your left as you descend south from the Cliff House, were originally used in the early twentieth century to help irrigate the park by pumping fresh water from oceanside springs. The Dutch Windmill (the complete one on the park's northwest corner) was completed in 1903. At that time it had a capacity of 30,000 gallons per hour.

The endeavor was such a success that in 1905 the Park Commission planned a second, the Murphy Windmill, donated by a wealthy banker named Samuel G. Murphy. But by 1913 the predominance of electricity made the windmills outdated. Once motorized water pumps were installed in the park, maintenance of the windmills dwindled.

For many years they stood neglected, weathered by fog and wind and subject to vandalism and damage by roosting birds. Then in 1981, Eleanor Rossi Crabtree, with volunteers from the Seabees Naval Reserve Unit, restored the Dutch Windmill to its architectural integrity. Now the sails turn, although the windmill does not produce power. The Dutch Windmill continues to function as a reference point for boats entering the Golden Gate, as it has since it was first built in 1903.

The Queen Wilhelmina Tulip Garden sits next to the Dutch Windmill. Tranquil and lovely, the garden is alive with color in the months of February and March, when 10,000 tulip bulbs bloom. *(John F. Kennedy Drive east of the Great Highway)*

In the late 1930s, the WPA Federal Art Project provided muralist Lucien Labaudt with a grant to paint the interior of the Beach Chalet. Labaudt was born in France in 1880 and moved to San Francisco in 1910. An early devotee of modern art in America, Labaudt experimented with surrealism and cubism in his painting. Labaudt's murals also appear at Coit Tower, on Treasure Island, and in Washington High School in San Francisco, as well as in the Paramount Theatre in Oakland and the U.S. Post Office and Court House in Los Angeles.

Like many artists of that era, Labaudt chose a theme that reflected the daily lives of common people. He painted in the classic fresco technique and was responsible for the overall design of the space, including the mosaics and woodwork. Over the years, although the Beach Chalet changed functions, the murals remained intact.

4 **BEACH CHALET** Now the site of a restaurant, microbrewery, and visitor's center, the Beach Chalet was the last project of architect Willis Polk. He designed this Spanish Colonial–style building in 1924 but didn't live to see its completion in 1925. Originally designed with amenities for visitors to Ocean Beach, the plan included a 200-seat restaurant on the second floor and a public lounge and changing rooms on the first floor.

During World War II, soldiers were housed in the Beach Chalet. After the war ended, the chalet was used as a social hall for the Veterans of Foreign Wars. In 1981 the building was closed. After a major renovation project in the late 1980s and early '90s, the Beach Chalet reopened in 1996 in its current incarnation.

Today, Lucien Labaudt's murals line the walls of the ground floor visitor's center, an informative and beautiful space. With displays on the history of Golden Gate Park as well as public rest rooms and an information officer, the visitor's center is worth a stop. At the restaurant upstairs, you can linger over a beer and one of the best burgers in the city while enjoying the exquisite oceanfront view. *(on the Great Highway south of John F. Kennedy Drive)*

5 **SAN FRANCISCO ZOO** Opened in 1929, the San Francisco Zoo has grown to nearly 70 acres of buildings and open space for about 1,000 animals, of which 130 are on the Endan-

The 1950s-vintage dog-head sign that was a beacon for visitors looking for the **Doggie Diner** (officially called the Carousel, 2750 Sloat Boulevard), across the street from the zoo, is considered a local landmark by a vocal contingent of nostalgic and kitsch-loving San Franciscans. They want to give it official landmark status, but the city has given it a limited lifespan. Catch it before the doggie disappears.

gered Species List. One of the few zoos in the United States to have koalas, it also has the famed Gorilla World, which, when it opened in 1980, was seen as a model for humane exhibition and care facilities. In the midst of growing controversy over the rights of captured animals, the zoo strives to meet the needs of the animals and the viewing demands from the public.

With a $48 million bond in hand, the zoo has set out on an ambitious plan to completely redesign itself into natural-habitat preserve. A new Latin American habitat and a Feline Conservation Center are already open, and a great ape forest, an African savanna with an elephant "range" exhibit, and other major new areas are planned or under construction. For now, though, visit the Insect Zoo, the Children's Zoo, the Koala and Penguin Crossings, and the feedings at the Lion House. *(Sloat Boulevard at 45th Avenue; 415/753-7080; www.sfzoo.org; open daily 10am to 5pm)*

6 LAKE MERCED A natural lake near the border of San Mateo County, Lake Merced is the only body of fresh water along the coastline between Point Reyes and Pescadero. It was once a favorite place for anglers, though in recent years the lake's water level has dropped significantly, diminishing the quality of fishing. Still, with concessionaires stocking the lake with trout, as well as limited numbers of naturally occurring catfish and black bass, anglers continue to come to Lake Merced. Bird-watchers have benefited from the lower water levels, which provide mud flats that attract shorebirds. More than a hundred species of birds live around Lake Merced, including marsh wrens, great blue herons, and double-crested cormorants.

The Boathouse Sports Club is a bar and restaurant that sometimes has live music. It sits directly above the boathouses for three rowing crews. The Pacific Rowing Club and the St. Ignatius Rowing Club are high school teams, and the Dolphin Club is an adult team. Occasional regattas are held on Lake Merced.

As you continue around the lake on John Muir Drive, you'll see (or hear) the Pacific Rod and Gun Club on your left. With trap, skeet, tower, and moving-target shooting, the club inhabits 14 acres on Lake Merced. Founded in the late 1920s, it is the only place in San Francisco where gun owners can legally shoot at fast-moving clay targets.

Walking or biking around Lake Merced is easy, since the path is relatively flat. A loop around both portions of the lake is about 5 miles and passes many of the sights listed in this segment. *(surrounded by Skyline Drive, John Muir Drive, and Lake Merced Boulevard)*

7 FORT FUNSTON Fort Funston served as a gun battery during World War II and as a storage site for Nike missiles in the early days of the Cold War. The three buildings near the parking lot were once Army barracks. They now house offices of the National Park Service. Stop by the ranger's office for information and assistance.

Today the coastal bluffs at Fort Funston are a favorite spot for dogs and their city-dwelling owners. There are two hiking trails here and access to the beach below. Venture down the Sunset Trail for a glimpse of the old Battery Davis. Restoration projects in some parts of the park are removing the non-native, though ubiquitous, ice plants and replacing them with native plants such as dune sagebrush and coast buckwheat. These efforts at restoring the habitat have brought increasing numbers of quail and bank swallows to nest at Fort Funston.

Thrill-seeking hang gliders soar in the skies here, providing visitors with an exciting spectacle. Each year, hang gliders and paragliders take off and land some 50,000 times at Fort Funston. Grab your windbreaker and settle into the bleachers above the beach for a show by these

A high school crew was rowing on Lake Merced when the 1989 Loma Prieta earthquake struck. The lake began to bubble, but the girls finished practice. Only after docking the boat an hour later did they learn the actual magnitude of what they figured was just a little quake.

History buffs may be interested to know that the yellow curbings in the Fort Funston parking lot cover the Nike missile silos sealed below.

daredevil folks, who strap a set of wings on their backs and then—no joke—jump off a cliff. *(Fort Funston visitor entrance on Skyline Boulevard ½ mile south of John Muir Drive; 415/239-2366)*

8 GOLF COURSES This segment of the Drive boasts four golf courses; the nine-hole Golden Gate Park Golf Course and the eighteen-hole Harding Park are municipally run, while the Olympic Country Club and the San Francisco Golf Club are private. For more information on booking tee times, contact the parks directly (Harding Park: 415/664-4690; Golden Gate Park Golf Course: 415/751-8987), or take a chance and just show up.

9 SAN FRANCISCO STATE UNIVERSITY Founded in 1899, San Francisco State University (SFSU) was originally called San Francisco State Normal School and offered a two-year training program for teachers. It was the first teaching college in the United States to require a high-school diploma. The school taught only women until its first male student registered in 1904.

Until the 1906 earthquake and conflagration, SFSU was located at Powell and Clay Streets on Nob Hill. Ten days after the quake, it reopened in temporary digs until a new site was found in the Haight-Ashbury District. It moved to its present location in the 1950s and was then known as San Francisco State College. This "new" campus is about 100 acres in size and serves about 25,000 students, both residents and commuters.

The campus has many performances that are open to the public, including a monthly chamber music series. The internationally known Poetry Center offers poetry readings. In this city, it is possible that one of these readers will be the next Allen Ginsberg or Marianne

Moore, both of whom read here in the center's early years. *(1600 Holloway Avenue at 19th Avenue; 415/338-1111; www.sfsu.edu)*

10 SIGMUND STERN MEMORIAL GROVE AND PINE LAKE The streams in this area feed the Laguna Puerca, a fishing pond next to the old Trocadero Inn, or "Troc," a raucous gambling establishment that was the scene of numerous gunfights. The best known of these occurred when a graft-taking politician named Abe Reuf was in a shootout with police at the entrance to the inn. The Troc has been rehabilitated twice, the first time by Bernard Maybeck, famed California architect, who left in place two bullet holes in the front door as a reminder of that police raid. Today, the Troc is called the Trocadero Clubhouse; it is the meeting place for a number of neighborhood groups.

In 1931, this beautiful setting with grass surrounded by fir, eucalyptus, and other trees was given to the city by Mr. and Mrs. Sigmund Stern. Sigmund Stern was a civic and business leader during the first two decades of the twentieth century. Mrs. Stern, who at the time was president of the Department of Recreation, donated the land with the stipulation that it be used for an ongoing festival of the arts. Its amphitheater was natural for such events. Today this park, dedicated to her late husband, is the likely spot to find your music-loving friends on a summer Sunday afternoon. Mrs. Stern also donated the laguna, now called Pine Lake, and its solitude and peacefulness are great for fishing, relaxing, and listening to a variety of birds singing. *(Stern Grove Music Festival: 415/252-6252, www.sterngrove.org; Stern Grove: Sloat Boulevard at 19th Avenue; Pine Lake: between Crestview and Wawona Streets west of Stern Grove)*

11 OUTER SUNSET Herb Caen's 1949 observation of "the little white new houses marching through the Sunset District toward the Pacific like stucco lemmings that decided, just in time, not to hurl themselves into the sea" still rings true today.

"The Sunset" refers to the area bounded by Golden Gate Park, the Pacific Ocean, Sloat Boulevard, and 7th Avenue. "The Outer Sunset" refers more specifically to the area west of 19th Avenue.

Sloat Boulevard, measuring 135 feet across, is San Francisco's widest street.

Since it was put on the map in the mid-twentieth century, the Sunset District has been San Francisco's urban suburbia. An abundance of single-family houses set on safe, quiet streets and surrounded by parks and ocean have given the neighborhood its reputation as a good place to raise a family.

Until Golden Gate Park was developed, what's now the Sunset District was a huge expanse of sand dunes, rolling from the Pacific Ocean to the foot of Twin Peaks. Even when construction on the park began in the 1870s, development in the surrounding neighborhood was very slow to take hold.

Sometime in the 1890s, the renegade community of Carville blossomed at the ridge of Ocean Beach. Several poor families bought outdated horse-drawn trolleys (which looked like cable cars) and moved them out to the beach, where they settled in and recycled the trolleys into homes. Carville was doomed in 1913 when neighborhood activists burned it down. Having no idea of the homeless problem that was to erupt many years later, then-mayor "Sunny Jim" Rolph said, "May San Franciscans never again be reduced to living under such miserable conditions."

Except for a couple of small communities, the Sunset was generally rugged and sparsely populated until a major building boom hit the neighborhood in the 1920s and 1930s. At that time, a developer named Henry Doelger built a number of stucco houses, and the Sunset came to be known as Doelger City. More projects followed, including a spate of row houses in the early 1940s, until all of the land in the Sunset was developed. Since then, the neighborhood has been home to an ethnically changing population of middle-class families, as Asian families have joined the longtime and mostly Irish residents.

There are several "main drags" in this area where you can go to shop, eat, or pick up on the diverse flavors that form the neighborhood: Irving Street, Taraval, and Noriega are all bustling with business. (For information on the Inner Sunset, see the Twin Peaks and Surroundings segment.)

DIRECTIONS

DRIVING

To continue the Drive from the previous segment (Point Lobos Avenue at the Cliff House): From the Cliff House, continue downhill (south) for 4 miles. Bear right as the Great Highway merges with Skyline Boulevard. At John Muir Drive, turn left (southeast). Follow John Muir Drive to its end at Lake Merced Boulevard. Turn left (north) onto Lake Merced Boulevard and follow as it curves around the lake, past San Francisco State University, to a right-turn lane (north) at Sunset Boulevard. Follow the turn lane onto Sunset Boulevard and continue to its end at Martin Luther King Jr. Drive in Golden Gate Park. (See page 125 for continued driving directions.)

PARKING

Parking is plentiful throughout this segment, with turnout parking along the Great Highway, parking lots at the Beach Chalet and Fort Funston, and street parking as well. The most difficult parking area is near San Francisco State University, especially when students are attending school.

BUS

The 18–46th Avenue bus, which starts in Lincoln Park and travels along Geary, will take you down the hill from the Cliff House and along the Great Highway as far as Lincoln Boulevard, the southern end of Golden Gate Park. It then travels on 46th Avenue to the zoo and onto Skyline Boulevard to rejoin the Drive, coming around Lake Merced to San Francisco State University. Here you must transfer at Winston Avenue at the north end of the campus to the 29–Sunset heading north on Lake Merced Boulevard. This bus then follows the rest of this segment of the Drive to Golden Gate Park. (See page 125 for continued bus directions.)

Polly Ann Ice Cream Parlor at 3142 Noriega Street sells 400 flavors of ice cream. The tiny store has space for only 50 flavors at a time, making frequent visits necessary for anyone who wants to taste all 400.

WALKING

In this segment, walkers should follow the driving directions.

GOLDEN GATE PARK

From Sunset Boulevard to Stanyan Street

GOLDEN GATE PARK

T his segment of the Drive travels from the rugged western end of Golden Gate Park to the cultural and developed eastern end. You'll see buffalo, horses, ponds, and meadows, as well as the Polo Fields where the original Summer of Love concert took place in 1967. Wind around Stow Lake—stop and rent a rowboat, or take a climb past the waterfalls to the top of Strawberry Hill—and continue past the arboretum. The Drive skirts the Music Concourse, which anchors art and science museums, and then passes the AIDS Memorial Grove, lawn bowling and tennis courts, and the track and field at Kezar Pavilion. A short detour will lead you to the Conservatory of Flowers, an exquisite greenhouse, or the Children's Playground, an enormous jungle of fun. This segment ends at the entrance to the Haight-Ashbury.

BEST WAY TO VISIT

Golden Gate Park is so large that you could spend your whole vacation in it without running out of things to do. We have listed telephone numbers and Internet web sites with information about specific attractions. For any other inquiries, call the park's general information number, 415/831-2700.

Look for the Explorer Pass for sale at most of the park's paid attractions. It gives discounts at the California Academy of Sciences, the Asian Art Museum, the Conservatory of Flowers, and the Japanese Tea Garden. For updated information about the Explorer Pass, call 415/750-7459. Discounts are also available for those holding valid Muni transfers and Fast Passes.

During the week, all roads (except construction detours) are open to automobiles. On Sundays, the park's main drive, John F. Kennedy Drive, is closed to cars from the Music Concourse to 19th Avenue.

THE DRIVE

GOLDEN GATE PARK OVERVIEW This great city park expanse, spoken of in the same breath as Central Park in New York, Hyde Park in London, and the Prater in Vienna, was once nothing more than sand. But through the combined visions of the city's civic leaders, the park's designer, William Hall, and his successor, John McLaren, Golden Gate Park has become an essential part of the city.

The park offers so many activities that we've broken our discussion of it into two parts, east and west. Essentially, the east is the urban part of the park, with buildings and other structures that attract most of the park's visitors. The western half is more rural.

The city designated this sandy land as a park in 1870. It was part of a settlement between the federal government and the city of San Francisco that determined the use and ownership of the lands outside of downtown, known as the Outside Lands or Outlands. San Francisco agreed to take 1,017 acres of the sandiest and least valuable land within the Outlands and give the rest to squatters and landowners. From this worthless land, a park would grow.

The city looked for help in the planning and development of such a difficult project. Frederick Law Olmsted, who had created New York's smaller Central Park out of 843 muddy, swamplike acres, came to look at this strip of land about 3 miles long and a half-mile wide. He was unable to see a way to make it work and declined the offer to design the park.

The mayor chose William Hall, an engineer who had worked on the federal surveying project for the Outside Lands. He quickly drew up designs for a park, was granted initial funding, and set out to make it happen. Planting first in the eastern half of the park, Hall used grasses such as barley that could grow in the sand and developed an irrigation system. He added shrubs and then trees, thus following nature's own path to developing ecological systems.

When a politically corrupt City Hall stole the money budgeted for the park, Hall quit the project. A number of years later, he was asked back — this time as a consultant. Before accepting, he made two demands: that he be hired for only one year and that he be allowed to appoint his successor. The person he chose to follow him was John McLaren, who, over period of 53 years from 1890 to 1943, brought the park's plans to fruition, fought City Hall to maintain the park's integrity, and enhanced the park with imported flora from around the world.

The Midwinter Exposition of 1894: In the early 1890s, a time of recession and bank panics throughout the nation, the city's leaders decided to hold a midwinter fair to stimulate the economy and enhance San Francisco's image throughout the world. It was a period of grandiose thinking on the part of people like M. H. de Young, publisher of the *San Francisco Chronicle,* and other business and banking leaders who desired to make San Francisco into "the Rome of the Pacific," according to Gray Brechin, the author of *Imperial San Francisco.*

The event was the first world's fair in California. Against the wishes of the park's leaders, the fair was held in the eastern part of Golden Gate Park, where buildings and a bandshell were erected. A tremendous success, with 37 countries participating and 2.5 million visitors, the Midwinter Exposition set the stage for the later fairs in San Francisco in the first half of the twentieth century.

1 GOLDEN GATE PARK WEST The Ocean Beach and the Sunset District segment described the westernmost edge of the park, including the windmills, the Beach Chalet, and the tulip garden. In this segment, the Drive enters the park about a mile east of its western border.

The Bercut Equitation Field, on the left (west) side after the turn onto Chain of Lakes Drive, is a training corral for horses and is used for small rodeos as well. The field was named for Golden Gate Park Commissioner Peter Bercut, a gardener and horseman who fought for horse use in the park.

After you turn right (east) onto John F. Kennedy Drive, you'll see the Buffalo Paddocks, containing about a dozen bison, on the left (north) side. The first bison, brought in 1894, were eventually wiped out by disease, and another group was brought in from Wyoming in 1984.

The Angler's Lodge and Fly-Casting Pools are one of those unexpected finds in the park. Hidden from the road and the polo field by trees and landscaping, these fly-casting pools are a secluded and quiet place in the ever-popular park. Casters come to practice, aiming for round targets placed at different points on the concrete ponds. The Angler's Lodge is a wood-and-glass building, reminiscent of a large cabin in the woods, used by the Angler's Association for meetings and special events. *(opposite the Buffalo Paddock on John F. Kennedy Drive)*

Spreckels Lake, a small lake on the Fulton Street side of the park, is the site of miniature sailing and radio-controlled yacht racing competitions and is also a congregating place for seniors and for many local Russian immigrants. *(near 36th Avenue and Fulton Street)*

The polo fields, also known as Golden Gate Park Stadium, are used for polo and other equestrian events, as well as football and soccer games. On the northern edge of the stadium are the Golden Gate Park Stables, where you can get a guided riding tour or riding lessons for a fee. *(415/668-7360; www.extend inc.com/ggps/; open daily 9am to 5pm)*

Yet the fields' greatest glory may have had nothing to do with horses at all. The summer of 1967, known as the Summer of Love, was as much an event in Golden Gate Park as it was on the streets of the Haight-Ashbury District. On these polo fields, the great rock groups of the late sixties—the Jefferson Airplane, the Grateful Dead, Janis Joplin with Big Brother and the Holding Company, Country Joe MacDonald, Jimi Hendrix, and many more—performed concerts. The polo fields continue to host a range of musical acts, from Van Morrison to the Beastie Boys.

On January 14, 1967, the first of the Human Be-ins—known as the "Gathering of the Tribes"—drew about 100,000 people and spilled out of the polo fields onto Speedway Meadow, a large, open expanse of green east and northeast of the stadium. Speedway soon became a regular meeting place for hippies and wannabes, drum beaters and guitar players, drug dealers and park police.

Today, the meadow is still a great place for Frisbee, golf, and just lying in the grass; it is a gathering place for families and often the site of large personal events such as weddings. Speedway is also the beginning and end point of the *Chronicle* Marathon, held in July. (For information, call 800-698-8699 or visit www.chroniclemarathon.com.)

Across from the eastern part of Speedway Meadow is Lloyd Lake, named for Reuben Lloyd, a former park commissioner. A small waterfall stands at the entrance, while toward the northwest corner of the lake are six Greek columns, all that was left of a mansion on Nob Hill after the

1906 earthquake and fire. A famous photograph called "Portals of the Past" shows them standing amidst the debris of a once-magnificent residential compound.

The columns reside here now so that their reflection in the waters will remind us of the vision of an ancient Roman past that San Francisco's early leaders attempted to emulate—a vision that was lost in the rubble of nature's devastation.

2 GOLDEN GATE PARK EAST Coming out of the relative wilderness of the western part of the park, the Drive crosses 19th Avenue (Cross Over Drive), the only north-south commuter route that cuts through the park. The eastern section of the park is filled with many attractions:

- Golden Gate Park has two lakes, Spreckels Lake in the western part and Stow Lake (Between John F. Kennedy Drive and Martin Luther King Jr. Drive at 17th Avenue) in the east. Stow's boathouse offers boat rentals by the hour or longer, including motor, row, and pedal boats. This is also the place to rent bicycles and group pedal carriages, purchase snacks, or use the bathrooms. *(415/752-0347; open daily 9am to 4pm, boats must be returned by 5pm; bicycle rentals from Surrey Bikes & Blades, 50 Stow Lake Drive, 415/668-6699)*

- The lake sits at the foot of Strawberry Hill, a wooded slope with a shady trail climbing to its summit. At the top are views of Huntington Falls, which feed Stow Lake below, and, to the north, of the golden domes of the Russian Church on Geary. At the bottom of Strawberry Hill, near where the falls flow into the lake on the western shore, is the Golden Gate Pagoda, a gift from the people of San Francisco's sister city, Taipei. The pagoda "commemorates the struggle and contribution of early Chinese settlers in California."

- Strybing Arboretum (between Martin Luther King Jr. Drive and Lincoln Way at about 9th Avenue) houses a collection of more than 6,000 plants and trees from all over the world that live in environments similar to that of the San Francisco Bay Area. Tours begin at the arboretum bookstore each day at 1:30pm. *(415/661-1316; www. strybing.org; open 8am to 4:30pm weekdays, 10am to 5pm weekends and holidays)*

3 **MUSIC CONCOURSE** The Music Concourse, situated between South Drive and John F. Kennedy Drive, is surrounded by the park's most popular attractions. The sunken, tree-lined esplanade, with its ornate band shell, was the focal point of the Midwinter Exposition held here in 1894. Today, concerts are often performed at the band shell, and amateur swing dancers sometimes practice on its stage. (For information on events, call the general information number for Golden Gate Park: 415/831-2700.)

On the south side of the Music Concourse is the California Academy of Sciences, including the Steinhart Aquarium, the Natural History Museum, and the Morrison Planetarium. Kids love the exhibits, and grown-ups are bound to learn something new while winding through the fish roundabout, shaking at the earthquake exhibit, or touring the universe in a sky show. *(415/750-7145; www.calacademy.org; open in winter 10am to 5pm, summer until 7pm; entrance fee, but free the first Wednesday of each month; additional fee for sky show at Morrison Planetarium)*

On the north side of the concourse are the de Young Museum, the Asian Art Museum, and the Japanese Tea Garden. The M. H. de Young Memorial Museum was given to the city by M. H. de Young, who, with his brother Charles de Young, founded the *San Francisco Chronicle*. It houses a collection of American art (largely from the John D. Rockefeller III collection) and a textile collection, as well as art from Africa, Oceania, and the Americas. The museum, closed while undergoing an extensive reconstruction, is scheduled to reopen in 2005. Shows originally planned for the de Young will be exhibited at the Palace of the Legion of Honor in Lincoln Park. *(415/750-3600 or 415/863-3330; www.thinker.org)*

The Asian Art Museum shares an entrance and admission fee with the de Young and is located in the building's west wing. Its extensive collection includes art from Tibet, China, Korea, Japan, India, Southeast Asia, and the Middle East. Although the de Young Museum closed in December 2000, the Asian Art Museum will stay open until it moves to the Civic Center area in 2002 (see the Civic Center segment).

(415/379-8801; www.asianart.org; open Tuesday to Sunday 9:30am to 5pm; fee, but free the first Wednesday of each month, when hours are extended to 8:45pm)

The Japanese Tea Garden is another relic from the time of the Midwinter Exposition. The exposition featured areas mimicking the look and feel of various foreign countries. What is now the tea garden was, during the exposition, the Japanese Village. It was such a popular attraction that the Park Commission decided to keep it in place after the fair was over, hiring landscape gardener Makoto Hagiwara to convert the village to a tea garden and expand its acreage.

Hagiwara and his family lived in a big house in the park, where they provided free room and board to new Japanese immigrants in exchange for their labor in building the tea garden. After Hagiwara's death in 1925, his family continued to run the garden until the beginning of World War II, when they were interned in Utah. But before they were evacuated, the Hagiwaras removed their collection of bonsai trees from the garden and left it with their friend Sam Newsom in Marin County.

When the war was over, Newsom sold the entire bonsai collection for the Hagiwara family to Dr. Hugh Fraser in Oakland. When Dr. Fraser's wife died in 1964, he honored her will and returned the bonsai trees to the Japanese Tea Garden. In addition to this collection, the tea garden now includes a bronze Buddha from 1790 and a "Lantern of Peace" from 1953, as well as a tea house, a pagoda, gates, bridges, several statues, a Zen stone garden, and 4 acres of peaceful grounds. *(415/831-2700; the gardens are free; fee for tea and snacks)*

Next to the Strybing Arboretum is the Shakespeare Garden, where samples of each of the flowers mentioned in the works of William Shakespeare grow. Other specialized collections, such as the Fuchsia Garden (summer- and fall-blooming), the Rhododendron Dell (March-blooming), and the Tree Fern Grove (year-round) are near the Conservatory of Flowers (see the Northeast Corner, below).

A grove of trees amidst a 7-acre plot, originally named the De Laveaga Dell, has become the National AIDS Memorial Grove. The only federally sanctioned memorial to those lost to Acquired Immune Deficiency Syndrome, established by a 1996 act of Congress, the dell is a secluded spot amidst the busy activities of the park. On the third Saturday of each month (except in winter), friends and family members of those who died of the disease come to work the soil by weeding, planting, and building this living memorial. *(415/750-8340)*

4 LAWN BOWLING Along Lawn Bowling Drive are a number of recreation areas. The lawn bowling area is to the southeast of the Music Concourse, and the tennis courts, where the late tennis champion Alice Marble played as a child, are adjacent to the bowling area. Nearby is the largest children's playground in the city and one of the oldest, having been established in 1887. Every city kid's favorite place to swing, slide, spin, and climb, this is no average playground. Even grown-ups will be amazed by all the fun to be had here. "Big Rec" has baseball diamonds and soccer fields for use by amateur leagues, as well as racquetball and handball courts.

Along the route as it leaves the park is a cozy pavilion/stadium called Kezar Pavilion. Built in 1922 and dedicated in 1925, it was designed by architect Willis Polk and named for members of the Kezar family, early San Francisco settlers.

The original Kezar Stadium had 60,000 seats. Its long history includes being the home of the San Francisco Forty-Niners until they moved to Candlestick Park in 1970. In 1989, Kezar Stadium was demolished and reconstructed as a 10,000-seat "pavilion" with an eight-lane running track and a World Cup–level soccer field. Today it is the site of local high school football and soccer games and track and field events.

The fortune cookie was invented in 1909 by Makato Hagiwara, the main gardener of the Japanese Tea Garden during the early 1900s. He introduced the cookies at the Midwinter Exposition, and they went on to achieve great popularity. Restaurants in Chinatown began to serve fortune cookies and later exported the recipe to China. The result, of course, is that the cookie we have come to know and love as a Chinese treat is in fact a San Francisco treat created by a Japanese man.

Golden Gate Park appears in *Star Trek IV: The Voyage Home* (1986). Orson Welles used the fish tanks at the Steinhart Aquarium in filming *The Lady from Shanghai* (1948).

5 **NORTHEAST CORNER** The **Conservatory of Flowers** is to the north and east of the Music Concourse. This wedding-cake-like greenhouse is the oldest building in Golden Gate Park and the oldest public greenhouse in California. When Hillary Rodham Clinton came to San Francisco in 1998, the then-First Lady called the conservatory "one of the most important landmarks in the country."

Millionaire James Lick intended to put the conservatory on his property in San Jose when he had it brought over from Ireland in 1876. But he died before it was delivered, and a group of businessmen, led by Leland Stanford, bought the greenhouse and donated it to Golden Gate Park.

Modeled after the conservatory in London's Kew Gardens, this "Richardsonian Romanesque" building was erected at its current location in 1878. For many years, it was filled with exotic plants and flowers, including one of the largest orchid collections in the world. Neglect and natural disasters have forced the park administration to close the conservatory.

The Recreation and Parks Department is restoring the conservatory and plans to reopen it in 2003. Tourists still flock to the grounds outside the closed building to admire the impressive structure and to enjoy the decorative flower beds in front—each bearing a timely greeting to the city.

Situated on the north side of John F. Kennedy Drive, just west of Stanyan Street, **McLaren Lodge** now houses offices for the Friends of Recreation and Parks. When it was built in 1896, following the design by Edward Swain, this Romanesque edifice became the home of John McLaren, the park's head administrator. In fact, McLaren lived here and managed the park until his death in 1943 at age 96.

If you're visiting San Francisco during the holiday season, try to catch the lighting of the colorful Christmas lights on the large cypress in front of McLaren Lodge. The ceremony has become a local tradition since McLaren requested the decoration of the tree when he was dying in 1943. Call the lodge (415/831-2700) for the exact date of the tree lighting, which usually takes place midweek during the second week of December.

Visitors to Golden Gate Park at any time of year can get information and maps at McLaren Lodge, open weekdays from 8am to 5pm, weekends from 8am to noon. For details on the free walking tours of Golden Gate Park led by the Friends of Recreation and Parks, see Walking in the Directions section below.

DIRECTIONS

DRIVING

To continue the Drive from the previous segment (Sunset Boulevard at Martin Luther King Jr. Drive): Turn left (west) onto Martin Luther King Jr. Drive. Turn right (north) onto Chain of Lakes Drive (this is the first stop sign—the street is unmarked). Turn right (east) onto John F. Kennedy Drive. At the corner just before the underpass beneath 19th Avenue (the only one on John F. Kennedy Drive), turn right (south) onto Traverse Drive, and then at the next stop sign take a soft left (southeast) onto Middle Drive. Continue to the next stop sign, and turn left (east) onto Martin Luther King Jr. Drive. Cross 19th Avenue (through the traffic light) and continue to Stow Lake Drive. Turn left (north) onto Stow Lake Drive, and then turn right (east) just after the boathouse. This is Stow Lake Drive East, which curves around the lake. At its end, make a sharp left turn (east) onto Martin Luther King Jr.

In the late 1960s the members of the Jefferson Airplane lived in the mansion at 2400 Fulton Street, on the northern edge of Golden Gate Park.

Drive. Follow it to Middle Drive, and then turn left (northeast). Where Middle Drive meets Lawn Bowling Drive, make a sharp right turn (south) and follow it to Martin Luther King Jr. Drive. Turn left (southeast) and continue to Kezar Drive. Turn left (east) onto Kezar and stay to the right (east), continuing onto Waller Street. Follow Waller to Stanyan. (See page 139 for continued driving directions.)

PARKING

Just about all of the curbside in Golden Gate Park, except directly in front of the buildings on the Music Concourse, is available for parking. The eastern end can get very crowded, especially on weekends, so be prepared to walk to exhibits in this area.

BUS

This is a segment to be done by car or on foot. No bus route mirrors the Drive within the park. In fact, the only buses within the park are those from the Richmond to the Sunset (and vice versa) that use a north-south route along 9th and 19th Avenues. (See page 140 for continued bus directions.)

WALKING

This is a great walking route. In this segment, walkers should follow the driving directions. There are also several free walking tours of Golden Gate Park run by the Friends of Recreation and Parks. Call 415/263-0991 for more information.

TWIN PEAKS & SURROUNDINGS

From the Haight-Ashbury to the Castro

VALENCIA ST

14TH ST
15TH ST
16TH ST
17TH ST

GUERRERO ST

22ND ST
23RD ST
24TH ST

CESAR CHAVEZ

DUNCAN ST

DOLORES ST

CHURCH ST

VICKSBURG ST

6

SANCHEZ ST

MARKET ST

18TH ST
19TH ST
20TH ST
21ST ST

LIBERTY ST

NOE ST

25TH ST
26TH ST
27TH ST

CASTRO

HARTFORD ST

HILL ST

ALVARADO ST

ELIZABETH ST

JERSEY ST

CASTRO ST

COLLINGWOOD ST

DIAMOND S

EUREKA ST

DOUGLAS S

5

STATES

HOFFMAN ST

CLIPPER ST

DIAMOND HEIGH

BUENA VISTA

ROOSEVELT

5

MARKET ST

BURNETT

CORBETT

MASONIC ST

HAIGHT

ASHBURY

ASHBURY ST

CLAYTON ST

COLE ST

17TH ST

FREDERICK ST

TWIN PEAKS BLVD

4

TWIN PEAKS BLVD

SKYVIEW WAY

PANORAMA DR

WALLER ST

STANYAN ST

PANORAMA DR

KEZAR DR

CARL ST

PARNASSUS AVE

1

CLARENDON AVE

PANORAMA DR

WOODSIDE

HUGO ST

CRESTMONT ST

WARREN ST

LAGUNA HONDA

3

JEWEY BLVD

5TH AVE
6TH AVE
7TH AVE

2

8TH AVE
9TH AVE
10TH AVE
11TH AVE

LAGUNA HONDA

ORTEGA ST

PACHECO ST

SAN MARCOS ST

IRVING ST

JUDAH ST

KIRKHAM ST

LAWTON ST

MORAGA ST

NORIEGA ST

QUINTARA ST

12TH AVE
FUNSTON AVE
14TH AVE
15TH AVE

INNER

SUNSET

LINCOLN WAY

N

TWIN PEAKS &
SURROUNDINGS

This section of the Drive guides you through the neighborhoods tucked along the southeastern corner of Golden Gate Park: the legendary Haight-Ashbury and the rapidly changing Inner Sunset. Passing the prestigious medical and dental school at the University of California at San Francisco, into the Inner Sunset District, the Drive heads south on 7th Avenue (which becomes Laguna Honda), past the picturesque reservoir, and comes around eucalyptus-covered Mount Sutro to follow the winding path up to Twin Peaks. At its summit, the lookout point atop the northern peak is truly one of the city's prized jewels—a 300-degree panorama of San Francisco. As the Drive drops down the northern side of the mountain, it passes through the Corona Heights neighborhood, where housing was built for the exquisite view. At the valley floor is the Castro District, San Francisco's capital of the gay and lesbian world.

BEST WAY TO VISIT

Although the 49-Mile Scenic Drive takes you along the Haight-Ashbury District, to see the sights of the Haight it is necessary to detour a few blocks east of Stanyan. If you want to explore these neighborhoods, we recommend that you park your car near the eastern end of Golden Gate Park and walk through the Haight-Ashbury.

The Drive also turns away before reaching the central spines of the Inner Sunset and, on the other side of Twin Peaks, the Castro, so you'll have to make a small diversion at each to get the feel of those communities. For the Inner Sunset, follow the Drive up Stanyan, go west on Parnassus, and park around 9th Avenue. After your walk, drive back to 7th Avenue to follow the rest of the Drive. The Drive passes the eastern edge of the Castro District as it crosses Market Street at 14th Street. To see the heart of this neighborhood, make a right on Market and proceed to Castro Street. You'll quickly see you're in the midst of it all.

One thing to keep in mind: Be prepared for heavy winds atop the Twin Peaks lookout point. Don't get caught without your jacket — and be forced into buying the sweatshirts that clever entrepreneurs sell to unsuspecting tourists.

THE DRIVE

HAIGHT-ASHBURY OVERVIEW Despite the stately history that preceded it and the thorny years that have followed it, the Summer of Love is what comes to mind for many when they think of the Haight. The Haight-Ashbury of the mid- to late 1960s was headquarters for everything the founders of the "new society" stood for — peace, freedom, and justice were as important as sex, drugs, and rock 'n' roll.

But long before the Haight became hippie central, it was a resort area for turn-of-the-century gentry—it was where wealthy San Franciscans built their country homes. Once the earthquake struck in 1906, the Haight-Ashbury, undamaged by the disaster, became populated by folks migrating west from downtown. The neighborhood flourished for some years but deteriorated during the Depression. Like the Western Addition, the Haight saw its population change again during World War II. African Americans who had moved to San Francisco to work in the shipyards and arms factories began moving into the Haight in the 1940s and 1950s.

Meanwhile, in North Beach, the Beats had become so well known that they were gentrifying their own previously inexpensive neighborhood. Newcomers to San Francisco seeking the beatnik life could no longer afford to live there. In the Haight-Ashbury, though, huge Victorian houses could be had for a song.

Beats who moved to the Haight from North Beach found a prominent youth culture in the San Francisco State University students who lived there. The Haight-Ashbury Beats made harsh decisions about what was cool: their black neighbors were hip, but the students were not. They denigrated the students as belonging to a lesser class of hip, and thus, according to one version of the word's genesis, were born the "hippies."

The Haight-Ashbury of the 1960s soon came to be dominated by these hippies, who are mostly remembered for bringing psychedelic drugs and outdoor rock concerts into the mainstream. Bands such as the Grateful Dead, Big Brother and the Holding Company, the Jefferson Airplane, Country Joe and the Fish, and the Charlatans were hugely popular and developed what came to be known as the San Francisco sound.

By the 1967 Summer of Love, the national media were hip to the Haight-Ashbury, and the news coverage attracted young people from around the country. The exuberant scene soon began to collapse, although the 1970s still brought to the neighborhood political activists and a youth culture intent on changing the world.

The Haight continued to evolve in the 1980s as gay clubs flourished in the neighborhood and the punk rock aesthetic took hold. By the 1990s, the rave scene was prominent—kids in baggy jeans passed party fliers on the corners, and techno music poured from the shops.

Haight Street today is as much a mainstream urban commercial strip as it is a gathering place for the weird. Fashion is predominant here, with trendy boutiques, vintage clothing shops, and stylish shoe stores peppering the blocks between Stanyan and Masonic. Reminiscent of Haight Street's heyday, smoke shops, record stores, and unusual bookstores also abound.

If you want to see the arts and performances the neighborhood has to offer, try to visit in mid-June, during the Haight Street Fair (call 415/661-8025 for the exact date). Otherwise, the best way to get a feel for Haight Street is to spend a few hours prowling through its nooks and crannies. Presented in the order you'll see them as you leave the park and head east on Haight Street, here are a few historic spots to check out:

- At the 49-Mile Scenic Drive's exit from Golden Gate Park stands the **Stanyan Park Hotel** (750 Stanyan Street at Waller), built in 1904. Now a National Historic Landmark, the hotel exemplifies what the area looked like when it was a turn-of-the-century resort.

- At 1775 Haight Street (still a private residence) was **the Diggers' crash pad**—the home base for the early radical organization that gave away free food in Golden Gate Park.

- Also dating from 1904 is the **Red Victorian Bed and Breakfast** (1665 Haight Street)—not to be confused with the art-house movie theater a few blocks down with the same name, **Red Victorian Movie House** (1727 Haight Street). Step into the lobby of The Red Victorian B&B to check out the psychedelic paintings by proprietor Sami Sunchild.

• Farther down Haight Street is the now-famous **Haight Ashbury Free Medical Clinic** (558 Clayton Street at Haight), founded in 1967 by Dr. David Smith. "Dr. Dave," as he is known, founded the clinic in preparation for the Summer of Love. What started as a refuge for flower children on bad trips has grown to an institution serving the medical, social, and psychological needs of 50,000 people a year. And, yes, it's still free.

• Continue down Haight another block and turn right on Ashbury. On the eastern side of the street is the **Grateful Dead House** (710 Ashbury Street); Jerry Garcia, Bob Weir, and Pigpen lived here in 1966 and 1967.

• Back down on Haight Street, continue to the corner of Masonic. The building at 1398 Haight (now a restaurant and brew pub) was once a hippie hangout called the **Drogstore Cafe**. The owners in 1967 wanted to call their business the Drugstore Cafe, but police found the name too provocative.

• Continue east on Haight and turn right on Buena Vista West (this will be a rather steep climb). At 737 Buena Vista West is the **Richard Spreckels Mansion**. Jack London wrote *White Fang* here, and Ambrose Bierce lived here toward the end of his life. In the 1960s the house became a popular spot with local musicians, as it then contained a small music-recording studio; Graham Nash lived here in the 1970s. Danny Glover bought the building in the 1990s.

• Return to Haight Street and continue another half block east. Turn left on Lyon Street—this is the block where **Janis Joplin** lived in 1967 and 1968.

1 UNIVERSITY OF CALIFORNIA, SAN FRANCISCO The mammoth development the Drive passes through on Parnassus is the esteemed University of California at San Francisco (UCSF). This prestigious hospital and medical school has been at this location since former mayor Adolph Sutro donated the 13 acres in 1898.

Today the campus encompasses 107 acres and includes 6 schools (medical, dental, nursing, pharmacy, psychiatry, and graduate research) as well as 11 research institutes, 1,500 laboratories, and more than 2,000 ongoing research projects. Researchers at the university play important roles in many aspects of medicine, especially in the fields of genetic engineering and biotechnology. Three UCSF researchers have won the Nobel Prize for Medicine. UCSF was the first medical center to establish a special care unit for people with AIDS and was among the first to identify HIV as the cause of the disease.

2 **INNER SUNSET** As you head west on Parnassus, the street becomes Judah at the intersection of 5th Avenue. This neighborhood west of the UCSF campus is the Inner Sunset—a hybrid community of medical students and middle-class families who have formed a quietly thriving village in their parkside locale. The neighborhood's hub is on 9th Avenue between Judah Street and Golden Gate Park (you'll head away from this area when the Drive turns left at 7th Avenue).

Located between the Outer Sunset and the Haight-Ashbury, the Inner Sunset is not as sleepy and foggy as the one nor as flamboyant and sunny as the other. The district is a microcosm of San Franciscan life, exuding a small-town feel and a mix of people and lifestyles. Asian groceries, used bookstores, high-end restaurants, and fashionable boutiques coexist here just south of Golden Gate Park.

Ninth Avenue—with its transfer points for many lines of public transit—bustles every day of the week; schoolchildren giggle on the corner while hurried professionals commute downtown. An abundance of cafes and restaurants beckon; many are strictly neighborhood favorites, though some have become destination points for the entire Bay Area. Le Video (1239 9th Avenue) is considered to have the city's best selection of cult and foreign films, while Ebisu (1283 9th Avenue) wins year after year in local polls as the city's best place to eat sushi. For cheap beer and good pizza, there's no place in the city like Milano's (1330 9th Avenue). Its display of turn-of-the-century photos of the neighborhood make this a destination interesting even for dieters.

Although most businesses here are owned by local folks, chain stores are creeping into the neighborhood. What was once a quiet mom-and-pop-shop strip is now transforming—for better or for worse—into a high-profile, trendy district.

3 **LAGUNA HONDA** As 7th Avenue heads uphill from Parnassus, the street name changes to Laguna Honda Boulevard, marking what was once a natural lagoon and is now a concrete-bottomed reservoir. To build Laguna Honda Boulevard, the city had to push back the mountain, so it erected a huge concrete retaining wall to keep the dirt from falling onto the road. Above the reservoir, to the left of Laguna Honda Boulevard, are the Laguna Honda Hospital and the Youth Guidance Center.

4 **TWIN PEAKS** While residents of cities like New York, Paris, and Chicago must travel to the tops of human-made structures for a view of the landscape of their metropolis, San Franciscans have Twin Peaks, a natural point that offers a stunning view of the San Francisco Bay Area. Without a doubt, this breathtaking vista rivals not only views in other cities but the great views at the Grand Canyon and other natural wonders.

The view is particularly impressive as the Drive climbs the southern side of Twin Peaks, where there are only occasional glimpses of what to expect on the eastern side of the lookout point. Mount Davidson, to the south and west of the peaks, is visible. Atop this 938-foot hill is a 103-foot-high concrete-and-steel cross where thousands of worshippers meet each Easter at sunrise. And there seems to be no escaping Mount Sutro to the northwest, with the red Communications Tower on its peak, visible from practically anywhere in the city.

Standing in the strong breeze at the lookout point and looking down at the city below, you can, on a clear day or evening, pick out some of the landmarks along the Drive: the Golden Gate Bridge, the Oakland Bay Bridge, City Hall, and Pacific Bell Park (a red structure contrasting with the basic whites or beiges of the houses and buildings of San Francisco). Golden Gate Park and the Presidio are to the north, and, with a slight turn of the head, you can see Buena Vista Park atop a nearby hill. Turn a little more, and there is the Transamerica Pyramid, looming over the Columbus Tower.

Then look northward again to Marin County; follow the compass around to Angel Island and Alcatraz and beyond them to the Richmond–San Rafael Bridge (the third of the four Bay Area bridges). Further along the arc is the Campanile, the clock-and-carillon tower on the University of California Berkeley campus. Look to the right of the campus on a clear day to see Mount Diablo, Alameda County's lookout mountain, in the background. Even with all of the stucco and brick, steel-reinforced concrete and glass, you can get an idea of what Gaspar de Portola's soldiers saw on their first sighting of the Bay Area from nearby Sweeney Ridge in Pacifica, nearly 230 years ago.

From here it is easy to see how compact the main part of the city is. Although the neighborhoods often feel isolated from one another, from here they can be seen as a continuous and contiguous arrangement.

5 **CORONA HEIGHTS/UPPER CASTRO** Also known as Upper Castro, Corona Heights was built at the base of Twin Peaks in the late 1800s and early 1900s. Originally the site of brickmaking factories that have long since disappeared, the neighborhood is built on streets that wind down to the Eureka Valley floor.

Corona Heights is now a fairly upscale area, with views of the city and the Bay Area. The neighborhood has a number of restored Victorian-style houses and gardens tended by the community. Follow Museum Way to its end to find the Randall Junior Museum, where children can learn about nature and science. Run by the San Francisco Recreation and Parks Department, the museum is also used by such diverse groups as the Audubon Society, the Golden Gate Model Railroad Club, and the San Francisco Hobby Beekeepers. *(199 Museum Way; 415/554-9600; www.randall.mus.ca.us; open Tuesday to Saturday 10am to 5pm; free)*

This area has a few beautiful stairway walks that take the walker up and down the side of the mountain. At Clayton and Iron Alley is a walkway that links to several other paths and walkways with equally breathtaking views of the city. (For those interested in the city's stairway walks, the definitive book on the subject is *Stairway Walks in San Francisco* by Adah Bakalinsky.)

6 THE CASTRO The Castro is world-renowned as a vibrant gay neighborhood. Since the 1970s, when thousands of gay men settled in what was then called Eureka Valley, the district has been home to the world's most out-and-proud homosexual contingent. In addition to the beautiful homes and eclectic shops that make up the Castro, the area has gained considerable political clout and boasts a quaint feel despite its fiercely radical history.

In the same way that the word "hippie" is associated with the Haight, the word "queer" is now associated with the Castro. As did the flower children in the Haight, gays in the Castro have made their neighborhood an international destination despite the fact that they are relatively recent settlers.

Most of the social life of San Francisco gays in the first part of the twentieth century was like that in other American cities—it took place late at night behind closed doors. In the mid-1950s San Francisco police instigated a series of crackdowns on gay hangouts, spurring gays to unite to create a community among the fragmented homosexual underground. Attracted by cheap housing and proximity to the cultural revolution in the Haight, gays began moving to the sunny slopes just on the other side of the hill.

Gays moved into Eureka Valley, restoring the dilapidated Victorians and beginning to establish America's first "gay hometown" around Castro Street. When gay merchants in the area were refused admittance to the Eureka Valley Merchants Association, they started their own group, the Castro Village Association, and the modern Castro was born. In 1964, *Life* magazine called San Francisco the "Gay Capital of the United States."

One man in particular gets credit for politically mobilizing the gay Castro. Harvey Milk was a New York stockbroker who moved to San Francisco to "be gay." He opened a camera store on Castro Street and, with his neighborly manner and political zeal, became known as "the Mayor of Castro Street." In 1977 Milk was elected to the San Francisco Board of Supervisors, the first openly gay elected official in California.

Although the neighborhood appeared to be thriving in the early 1980s—real estate was expensive, shops were busy, and community spirit was strong—AIDS had arrived and was wreaking havoc on the Castro. By 1990, 10,000 people in San Francisco had died of AIDS.

The Castro today is an amalgam of gay cultures. Some of the men who settled here in the 1970s are still around, though as the male population declined in the 1980s many lesbians began moving to the neighborhood. Families also live in the Castro. The real estate remains pricey, and the streets still bustle. The activism of the younger generation—with groups like LYRIC and ACT-UP—has led to a broadened acceptance of different lifestyles. Loudly proclaiming their "queer" identity, young gays, lesbians, and transgender people of various ethnicities have transformed the Castro from a haven for middle-class gay white men to a community celebrating its diversity.

The best way to enjoy the Castro is to explore its main corridors: eclectic shops and excellent people-watching abound along Market, Castro, and 18th Streets. Or take a seat in one of the many outdoor or window-fronted restaurants, bars, and cafes, and watch the sights go by. Although most of the action here is simply in the people who make up the neighborhood, there are a few important sights to check out:

- Twin Peaks (401 Castro Street at Market). When it opened in the 1970s, Twin Peaks was the first gay bar in America with windows facing the street—a significant symbol of the emergence of gay life into the mainstream.

- Castro Theater (429 Castro Street). This elaborate Spanish Renaissance movie theater opened in 1922 and has been a booming business ever since. The Castro specializes in unusual films—art films, vintage classics, and theme-oriented film festivals. The Gay and Lesbian Film Festival is held here, as are the Jewish Film Festival and the Animation Festival. In addition to its fine films, the Castro boasts a pipe organ (still played before most screenings) and an ornately decorated interior.

- A Different Light Bookstore (489 Castro Street). Specializing in books by, about, and for gays, lesbians, bisexual, and transgender people, this store is a great resource for finding out what's going on in the gay community. You can also get information here about the "Cruising the Castro" walking tour, guided by Castro resident Trevor Hailey.

• Harvey Milk Plaque. At 575 Castro Street, the location where the "Mayor of Castro Street" had his camera shop and lived in an apartment above, is a plaque commemorating Harvey Milk.

• Names Project. Forming the AIDS Memorial Quilt, the Names Project assembles tens of thousands of handmade panels, each representing a person lost to AIDS. (415/863-1966)

• The Castro is the site of a number of annual fairs and festivals. The Castro Street Fair takes place the first Sunday in October. Easter is often celebrated in the Castro with skits by the Sisters of Perpetual Indulgence—a troupe of drag queens dressed as nuns. The Castro's biggest party of all is on the night of Halloween. Not always in the Castro District, but largely attended by the gay community, are the Gay Lesbian Bisexual and Transgender Pride Parade on the last Sunday in June and the Folsom Street Fair on the last Sunday in September.

DIRECTIONS

DRIVING

To continue the Drive from the previous segment (Waller Street at Stanyan): Turn right (south) from Waller onto Stanyan. At Parnassus (four blocks), turn right (west) and follow it seven blocks to 7th Avenue. Turn left (south) onto 7th Avenue, which becomes Laguna Honda. Continue on Laguna Honda, past the enormous retaining wall overlooking the reservoir, about 1.5 miles. At Woodside, turn left (east) for a half mile. At the top of the hill, turn left (northeast) onto Portola Drive. Almost immediately, there is a left-turn lane to Twin Peaks Boulevard. Take that left (north) onto a winding uphill road. This part of the route is clearly marked. Follow the sign at the top of the hill to the lookout point. When leaving the lookout area, turn right and right again to head downhill. Turn right (east) onto Clarendon. At Clayton, turn left (north), and then turn right (east) onto 17th Street. At Roosevelt, turn left (northeast), and continue to 14th Street. Turn right (east) onto 14th Street and head to the bottom of the hill to Market Street. (See page 152 for continued driving directions.)

PARKING

The Haight and the Inner Sunset are densely packed residential areas, so street parking is difficult. In the Haight, you can pay for parking at Kezar Pavilion—enter on Stanyan near Beulah. Some stores along Haight Street validate parking in this lot. There are two small parking lots in the Inner Sunset: one on 6th Avenue between Irving and Judah and another on 8th Avenue between Irving and Judah.

Twin Peaks offers parking at the lookout, where, depending upon the time of day and the season, there are usually places to park. The Randall Junior Museum has some parking as well. The Castro relies on metered parking in its business district.

BUS

Walk from Waller on Stanyan south four blocks to Parnassus. To go from the Inner Sunset to Twin Peaks via 7th Avenue, take the 43–Masonic on Parnassus to Woodside and transfer to the 44–O'Shaughnessy to reach Portola Drive. From there walk one block to Twin Peaks Boulevard and start walking uphill to the top of Twin Peaks. Walk down the north side of Twin Peaks Boulevard to Clayton and Corbett to catch the 37–Corbett to 14th Street and Market. (See page 152 for continued bus directions.)

WALKING

This 6½-mile segment is long and mostly uphill, with a steep downhill slope from Twin Peaks. And walking along Laguna Honda can be a bit treacherous. It's best to walk around the Haight and the Inner Sunset Districts and then catch the 43–Masonic bus up to Laguna Honda at Woodside, where the Laguna Honda Medical Center is. From there the uphill walk has sidewalks to keep you out of traffic, and then it follows the less busy (but without sidewalks) Twin Peaks Boulevard to the summit peak.

After reaching the lookout point, descend Twin Peaks Boulevard to the north and east to Clarendon. Make a right turn (east) onto Clarendon and walk to Clayton. Turn left (north) onto Clayton, and then turn right (east) onto 17th Street. Partway down is Roosevelt, where a left turn (north-northeast) leads to the Roosevelt Park dog area and to the Randall Junior Museum. Follow Roosevelt's curves to 14th Street, where a right-turn merge (east) will take you to the valley floor. The Castro District, however, is easier to approach from 17th Street, which takes you to its center.

THE MISSION

From Upper Market to the Interstate 280 Freeway

THE MISSION

The Mission District has one of the richest histories among San Francisco neighborhoods—it was here that Spaniards first settled San Francisco, enslaving Ohlone people to build the mission and converting them to Christianity. After many transformations, the Mission District today offers up an interesting melange of cultures. The neighborhood is at once the city's most visible Latin American community and a bastion for young bohemians, painters, and dot-commers alike. The sights, sounds, and smells along 24th Street reveal the Latino heritage of the Mission, while a visit to the boutiques and restaurants along Valencia Corridor shows how trendy the neighborhood has become.

As the Drive takes you south on Dolores Street—past the miles of palms that make this undulating road so pretty—it passes San Francisco's oldest monument and the neighborhood's namesake: the

Mission Dolores. Continuing past sunny Dolores Park, you'll glimpse the picturesque Victorian and Edwardian homes along Dolores before turning onto Cesar Chavez Street (formerly Army Street). Here you'll see the proletarian homes of the eastern side of the Mission District before continuing on to the industrial section of town. This segment ends at the Cesar Chavez Street freeway entrance to Interstate 280 north.

BEST WAY TO VISIT

This part of the Drive follows two major thoroughfares and therefore is easy enough to follow. However, to get a feel for the truly colorful neighborhoods that these streets surround, we recommend making detours into the Mission, Noe Valley, and Potrero Hill Districts to see the sights not directly on the Drive.

THE DRIVE

MISSION DISTRICT OVERVIEW The history of the Mission Dolores sets the stage for an understanding of the history of the neighborhood as a whole—and to a large extent exemplifies the history of California in general. Since the Mission Dolores was built over 200 years ago, the neighborhood that grew around it has been home to immigrants and invaders, refugees and conquerors.

In the mid-nineteenth century, working-class German and Scandinavian immigrants populated the Mission District. When the earthquake destroyed downtown neighborhoods in 1906, many Irish and Italian Americans moved into the Mission, bringing with them a new way of speaking, an accent specific to the "Mish." Latinos were present in the Mission in small numbers even in the early twentieth century. Some came to vacation in San Francisco, and many others came to work for the fruit companies and coffee roasters doing business here.

In the 1950s, immigration from Latin America began to rise significantly. By 1970, Latinos made up 45 percent of Mission District residents; by 1990, they constituted 52 percent. The cultures of Mexico, Nicaragua, Guatemala, and El Salvador are some of the many you'll see represented in the Mission.

In the late 1960s and early 1970s, the cultural revolution that swept the rest of the country also hit the Mission. The Latino community was staunchly raising consciousness about "La Raza" and the socioeconomic realities of immigrants and indigenous people. Part of this effort involved painting murals in the neighborhood that reflected life-affirming messages. Murals had long been a part of Mexican culture, and, as immigration from Mexico increased and pride in cultural heritage swelled, mural painting in the Mission became ubiquitous. This movement started a trend that still thrives today—you'll see these vibrant images on surfaces throughout the neighborhood.

In the 1980s, bohemian life moved into the Mission, as non-Latino artists converged on the cheap housing and large industrial spaces. Lesbians began congregating in the Mission in the mid-1970s. By the 1980s they had established a thriving presence along Valencia Street that still lives on today in the many women-oriented bookstores, erotic shops, and bathhouses throughout the neighborhood. The **Women's Building** (3543 18th Street; 415/861-8969), for instance, was established in 1971. Covered with a gorgeous mural, the building houses a number of nonprofit organizations serving women and families.

Despite these influences, the Mission remained largely Latino and working class—at least through the 1990s. However, as was true in the Haight and in North Beach before it, the Mission District has become an increasingly hip place to live as well as a nightlife scene visited by people throughout the Bay Area. As property values have skyrocketed throughout the city, the Mission has undergone major gentrification. High-end dining and retail establishments line Valencia Street, while dot-com companies have moved into warehouses east of Mission Street.

1 DOLORES STREET As soon as you turn onto Dolores Street, you'll notice something special. Huge palms line the median of this wide thoroughfare, planted in 1910 by John McLaren, then the chief administrator of Golden Gate Park. (You'll also notice that cars are parked perpendicular to the median, another of the street's peculiarities.)

Dolores Street was an important marker even before the palms went up. The fire that followed the great earthquake of 1906 was thwarted at Dolores Street, saving the neighborhoods west of it from the damage that ruined downtown. Because of the "firewall" created at Dolores Street, the houses west of it are generally intact Victorians, while those east of it are of the later Edwardian era.

2 MISSION DOLORES The mission here is named *dolores*, the Spanish word for sorrows and pain. But the fact that the neighborhood's residents—from the indigenous Ohlone Indians that once inhabited the area to the present-day communities of radical artists and Latin American immigrants—have been subjected to much sorrow and pain by the mainstream society is perhaps a historical coincidence.

Originally called the Missión San Francisco de Asís, Mission Dolores (its more colloquial name) is the oldest building in San Francisco still standing. (The Commandante's Quarters at the Presidio was built first, but only its foundation remains; see the Presidio segment.) The Mission was founded in 1776 as part of Spain's effort to settle Upper (*Alta*) California and convert the native people to Christianity.

Because the rugged, windy landscape along the coast where the Presidio was established was undesirable as a mission location, the settlers explored inland and soon came upon an ideal setting—a sheltered valley beside a stream-fed freshwater lagoon. They found the location on the Friday before Easter—the Friday of Sorrows—and therefore called their settlement *Laguna de los Dolores*. They built a simple shelter of branches and held mass here on June 29, 1776. This event, just days before the new nation declared its independence, is considered the beginning of modern San Francisco.

But when the Spanish settled on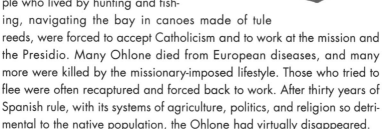
the lagoon, they also began
to enslave the Ohlone Indian
Nation that had inhabited the
land for thousands of years.
The Ohlone, a peaceful people who lived by hunting and fish-
ing, navigating the bay in canoes made of tule
reeds, were forced to accept Catholicism and to work at the mission and
the Presidio. Many Ohlone died from European diseases, and many
more were killed by the missionary-imposed lifestyle. Those who tried to
flee were often recaptured and forced back to work. After thirty years of
Spanish rule, with its systems of agriculture, politics, and religion so detri-
mental to the native population, the Ohlone had virtually disappeared.

The temporary structure used for worship in 1776 was replaced in the
1780s with the permanent building that still stands today. Ohlone Indians built the mission, while Franciscan friars oversaw their work. In 1833
the Mexican government took over the chapel (Mexico had conquered
California in 1821 during its revolt against Spain), but it didn't spend
any resources on its upkeep. During the gold rush era, however, newly
settled fun-loving San Franciscans spiffed up the mission and used it as a
venue for (what else?) drinking and gambling. In 1857 the mission was
restored to more pious uses when the Catholic Church once again took
control of it. Since then it has been a place of worship, though it has
undergone several restorations and additions.

Visiting the Mission Dolores is easy and informative—and not a very
crowded stop on the tourist circuit, given its great historical significance.
Enter through a small door to the left of the main church entrance. See
the chapel, basilica, museum, and cemetery. Make sure to look up when
you visit the chapel—the ceiling here is the most unusual feature, fash-
ioned after the basket designs of the indigenous people who built it.
*(3321 16th Street at Dolores; 415/621-8203; open daily 9am to 4pm;
donation requested)*

3 **DOLORES PARK** Two blocks south of the Mission Dolores
lies the oasis of Dolores Park, on land that was a Jewish cemetery
from 1861 to 1905. Situated in one of the sunniest corners of

A gold fire hydrant at 20th and Church Streets gets a new coat of paint each year when neighbors pay tribute to the pump that saved the neighborhood from the 1906 post-earthquake fire that was creeping toward the area from downtown.

San Francisco and replete with tennis courts, basketball courts, a playground, expansive rolling fields, and exquisite views, this park is well loved by city residents. Look in local newspaper events calendars for free music and theater performances here on summer weekends.

Climb to the park's southwestern corner (Church and 20th Streets) for a panoramic view of downtown San Francisco. Also known as "Dolores Beach" among the many residents who enjoy sunbathing here, Dolores Park is popular with residents of the nearby Castro District. Across the street from the park (on 18th Street between Dolores and Church) is Mission High School, built in the 1920s in the Mission Revival style with crisp white walls and a red tile roof. *(between Dolores, Church, 18th, and 20th Streets)*

4 VALENCIA CORRIDOR For better or for worse, the gentrification of the Mission is most obvious along Valencia Street from 16th Street to 24th Street, an area so yuppified it's now called a "corridor" instead of a street. Look here for bars drowning in hipsters, shops selling the latest fads in furniture, clothing, or eyeglasses, and restaurants teeming with foodies. Alongside these newer establishments are an array of more classic shops—funky bookstores, women-oriented businesses, and, of course, plenty of taquerias.

Levi's jeans were invented in California in the mid-nineteenth century. Their inventor patented the sturdy pocket rivets at a time when gold diggers were busy filling their pants with the heavy yellow stuff. Still turning out the extra-strength denim (though the pockets these days are more likely to be stuffed with plastics than with minerals), **Levi Strauss** opens its smallest and oldest factory to the public during its weekly tour. *(250 Valencia Street between 14th and 15th; 415/565-9153 or 415/565-9159 for reservations and information)*

One of the first female/lesbian erotic stores in the nation was Joni Blank's **Good Vibrations**; it is still going strong, offering quite a variety of sexual toys and aids. Stop in to see her Museum of Antique Vibrators, with items dating back to 1869. Oh, those Victorians! *(1210 Valencia Street; 415/974-8980; www.goodvibes.com)*

5 MISSION STREET In his failed run for mayor in 1999, former mayor and police chief Frank Jordan observed that Mission Street looked "like a bombed-out section of Beirut." A clever journalist at the time pointed out that Jordan's comment "suggests he has spent little time recently in either place." It's true that a stroll down Mission Street doesn't reveal the new wave of prosperity that has graced Valencia Street just one block west. However, on this bustling urban street you'll find lots of families and a blend of bohemian, Asian, and Latino cultures—dive bars and hip lounges, Mexican restaurants and Chinese seafood, and more schlock shops than you can count.

6 24TH STREET This part of the Mission is still heavily Latino—a walk down 24th Street from Mission Street to Potrero Street will surely test your Spanish and your knowledge of Latin American culture. Here you'll find dress shops specializing in *quinceañera* gowns, gift shops with Catholic relics and saints' candles, produce markets selling cactus, plantains, and a variety of chile peppers, *panaderías* with their pretty breads and pastries, and record stores carrying more mariachi, Tejano, and rock-en-Español than hip-hop, jazz, or punk.

Galería de la Raza (2857 24th Street, 415/826-8009) shows rotating exhibits of contemporary Latin American art; the adjacent **Studio 24** sells crafts made by local Latin American artists. **The Mission Cultural Center** (2868 Mission Street, 415/821-1155) hosts performances and concerts as well as classes and rotating art exhibits.

For freshly made ice cream or candy, stop by the **St. Francis Fountain and Candy Shop** (1024 24th Street). They've been serving up tasty treats to neighborhood residents for more than eighty years. Articles posted inside the pink-and-white ice cream parlor say that the San Francisco Forty-Niners football team was created here.

Casa Sanchez (2778 24th Street) got a lot of media attention when it offered free food for life to all those who tattooed its little "corn man" logo anywhere on their bodies. Regardless of whether you opt for the art, the food, the price, or the charming outdoor courtyard, Casa Sanchez is worth a stop for the classic Mission burrito.

For a particularly dense concentration of murals, visit **Balmy Alley** (between 24th and 25th Streets). The cultural institutions that nurture this artistic flair are also well worth a visit. **Precita Eyes Mural Arts and Visitors Center** (2981 24th Street, 415/285-2311) offers slide shows and walking tours of the Mission District's murals.

7 **NOE VALLEY** When José de Jésus Noé, the last *alcalde* (mayor) of Yerba Buena under Mexican rule, sold his vast holdings to John M. Horner in 1854, the new owner subdivided the land, naming a portion of the property in honor of Noé. Inaccessible from downtown until the Market Street Cable Railway brought the cable car up Castro Hill, the area consisted of small dairy farms. Transportation brought working- and middle-class German and Scandinavian immigrants, who settled in small homes. Later, Irish Americans joined the mix. As in other neighborhoods in this area, the post–World War II flight to the suburbs brought a major decline to home values in Noe Valley. The area came back as the 1970s skyscraper boom in downtown brought office workers back into the city. A new generation of residents bought and refurbished homes in the area, making Noe Valley a vibrant neighborhood.

Noe Valley is bounded by 22nd and Cesar Chavez Streets and Eureka and Dolores Streets. Its town center is 24th Street, with a number of coffeehouses, bookshops (try Phoenix Books), and boutiques. All in all, the area has once again become a family neighborhood, albeit upper middle class. Baby strollers abound, and kids line up for ice cream at the local parlor.

8 **POTRERO HILL** Even with some of the best views of downtown and the bay in all of San Francisco, Potrero Hill was a neglected part of town until the last decade of the twentieth century. With heavy industry on two sides of the hill and its location between two freeways, the area was pretty isolated from the rest of the residential communities in this city. A Russian émigré community at the turn of the century, Potrero Hill next became known as an artists' colony, its small cottages and the views from the hilltop (along with cheap rents) attracting those with "an eye."

Today, Potrero Hill has become another turnaround neighborhood where younger professionals have come to seek refuge. With each refurbished home the area's housing value grows by leaps and bounds. Ironically, it is also the home to public housing projects, creating a diverse mix of economic and social lifestyles.

To see Potrero Hill, from Cesar Chavez Street, just as you reach the Interstate 280 overpass, turn left (north) onto Pennsylvania and follow it to 18th Street. Turn left (west) onto 18th and follow it to Connecticut. This area is the shopping district, with a mix of old stores and new restaurants. One of the longtime coffeehouses is **Farley's** (1315 18th Street). See the tapestries and stained glass decor at **Eliza's Hunan and Mandarin Restaurant** (1457 18th Street).

Head up Connecticut and take a right onto 20th Street. The view of downtown from inside the **Potrero Hill Public Library** (1616 20th Street) remains magnificent. Backtrack two blocks to the corner of Texas and 19th Streets to see the house used in exterior shots for the 1990 movie *Pacific Heights*, starring Michael Keaton and Melanie Griffith. The set on Potrero Hill is actually clear across town from the neighborhood where the film supposedly takes place.

The **Potrero Hill Neighborhood House** was built in 1908 and designed by Julia Morgan, one of California's finest architects. The Potrero Hill Theatre is housed in this building. *(953 De Haro at Southern Heights Street)*

Need to see the steam-brewing method of local beer making? Stop in at the **Anchor Steam Beer Brewery.** Small group tours are held at 2pm, but you must reserve well in advance. *(1705 Mariposa Street at De Haro; 415/863-8350)*

At one time, one of the **Wisconsin Street** blocks was the home to such writers and artists as Lawrence Ferlinghetti and Lucy Coons. Another Wisconsin block will put your heart in your throat as you drive down one of the steepest slopes in the city.

Stop by **Baby Park**, as it is known, at 20th and Vermont and try the swings in the playground. The park cliff faces west toward Twin Peaks and the omnipresent Mount Sutro; while swinging, you may get the feeling that, were you to let go, you might fly right off the cliff. Don't worry; you won't. Looking down the cliff you see the tops of the buildings in the San Francisco General Hospital complex (1001 Potrero Street, between 22nd and 23rd Streets). So should you fall, help really is nearby.

From there, head south (away from downtown) on **Vermont Street** to experience the actual crookedest street in the city, regardless of what the tourist bureau says about Lombard Street. Vermont's curves are sharper; notice also the well-tended gardens. It has, however, one less turn than Lombard. Leave the area by following Kansas, turning right onto 26th Street at the bottom of the hill. As the road curves, it once again becomes Vermont Street. Follow it back to Cesar Chavez Street. Turn left to rejoin the 49-Mile Scenic Drive.

DIRECTIONS

DRIVING

To continue the Drive from the previous segment (14th Street at Market): Cross Market Street on 14th Street eastbound, continue one block, and turn right (south) onto Dolores Street. Follow Dolores seventeen blocks to Cesar Chavez Street. Turn left (east) and follow it 2 miles to Indiana (just past the second freeway overpass). Turn left (north) onto Indiana to the northbound entrance to Interstate 280. (See page 164 for continued driving directions.)

PARKING

Parking in these neighborhoods is generally at one-hour meters or in two-hour residential areas. The one exception is the city-owned Mission Bartlett Garage, at 90 Bartlett Street, near 21st Street and between Valencia and Mission Streets.

BUS

None of the city's bus lines follow the Drive in this area. However, you can use the following buses to visit the sights and neighborhoods listed in this segment: Catch the J–Church streetcar at 14th Street and Market, getting off at 16th Street to visit Mission Dolores and Dolores Park, one block east. Then hop back on and continue to 24th Street. Use the 48–Quintara bus heading west (uphill) on 24th to visit Noe Valley, and the 48–Quintara east (downhill) to visit the Mission District and Potrero Hill. The 48–Quintara continues east to 22nd and 3rd Streets, where it meets the bus for the next segment, 15–3rd Street. (See page 165 for continued bus directions.)

On the **Potrero Hill Recreation Center** at Arkansas and 23rd Street is a four-paneled mural honoring, among others, O. J. Simpson, the once-local hero, for his athletic abilities.

WALKING

In this segment, walkers should follow the driving directions. However, instead of entering the freeway, as the Drive does here, walkers should make the following accommodations: At Indiana Street and the Interstate 280 North entrance, continue on Indiana about five blocks to 22nd Street. Turn left to go two blocks to the CalTrain station at Pennsylvania. Or turn right to go four blocks to 3rd Street to catch the 15–3rd to continue on in the next segment.

EASTERN WATERFRONT

From Mission Bay to the Ferry Building

EASTERN WATERFRONT

This segment of the Drive highlights an area of San Francisco that is undergoing significant change. Once a destitute industrial zone, the areas called South Beach and Mission Bay—bordered by 16th Street, Brannan Street, the US 101 freeway, and the bay—are in the process of vast revitalization. While South Beach is close to being finished, Mission Bay to the southwest is just beginning its changes, expected to take as long as thirty years.

The first sight on this segment of the Drive is the awesome downtown San Francisco skyline—visible as you head north on Interstate 280. When the Drive exits the freeway just a mile and a half later, it passes the quirky houseboat community on Mission Creek before approaching the beautiful Pacific Bell Park, home of the San Francisco Giants. Continuing along King Street, the drive skirts "Multimedia Gulch"—the city's version of high-tech Silicon Valley—and then heads along the Embarcadero, where you'll soak up the new spirit of this stretch of waterfront, before concluding at the Ferry Building, the historic anchor of this neighborhood in flux.

BEST WAY TO VISIT

This portion of the Drive includes about 1.5 miles on the freeway. Pay attention to rush hour traffic from 4 to 7pm on weekdays. The traffic in the downtown area is usually at a crawl at that time. If there is a baseball game at Pacific Bell Park, expect extra traffic as well.

The King Street/Embarcadero part of the Drive is easy to walk, and the N–Judah streetcar line that travels from the Outer Sunset ends its route aboveground at 3rd and Townsend, next to Pacific Bell Park.

A couple of things to keep in mind in this area: Piers south of the Ferry Building have even numbers, those north of the Ferry Building have odd numbers. Also, signs for the 49-Mile Scenic Drive may be hard to see—they sometimes appear on the left side of the street in these parts.

THE DRIVE

1 **VIEW OF DOWNTOWN FROM INTERSTATE 280 NORTH** The skyline of San Francisco is magnificent from Interstate 280; from Market Street to the north, skyscrapers abound, hiding the San Francisco–Oakland Bay Bridge, the Ferry Building, and the Embarcadero from view. It is hard to see the notable buildings of the Financial District (such as the Transamerica Pyramid and Embarcadero

Center) from here, but most of the downtown buildings were built in the 1970s when the city went through an office-construction frenzy. Today the city's physical image befits its economic importance. It has gone from being just a regional center of commerce and banking to a world capital.

2 **MISSION CREEK AND THE HOUSEBOATS** As you exit Interstate 280 and drive east on King Street, a glance to your right reveals Mission Creek and the houseboats that are berthed there. Although the strip has the look of a hasty afterthought in city planning, Mission Creek is in fact often overlooked in the founding of San Francisco. Some 5,000 years ago, the area's first inhabitants, the Ohlone Indians, lived in small villages around Lake Merced and Mission Creek. When the Spaniards came to settle California in the eighteenth century, they built their mission in a valley beside a lagoon that was fed by Mission Creek. (See the description of Mission Dolores in the Mission segment.)

Today, the creek looks more like a canal, and the only "Indians" you'll see around here are the motorcycles that belong to the houseboats' inhabitants. This bohemian community has been on Mission Creek since at least the 1960s, though gleaning historical information about it is difficult since almost nothing is documented about the offbeat houseboat "neighborhood." For a close-up look at the creek and the houseboats, turn right off King onto 4th Street, cross the small bridge, and then turn right onto Channel. At the end of Channel, near 6th Street, there is a parking area. From here you can enjoy a walk in the small park along Mission Creek.

3 **MISSION BAY** The open land that stretches south from the King Street off-ramp was once a rustic spread of rail yards and warehouses. Since the 1970s, San Francisco has been in the process of deciding what to do with this privately owned waterfront land. The end result of thirty years of negotiations between environmentalists, developers, housing activists, and politicians is a 303-acre work in progress called Mission Bay. ("Mission Bay" refers, more or less, to the land bounded by 7th and 16th Streets and by Townsend Street and the bay.) In progress in Mission Bay is the construction of a second campus for the University of California

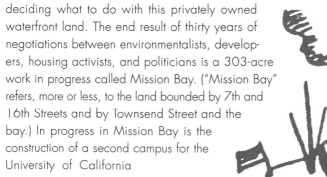

San Francisco. Housing, shops, a school, and acres of open space will be developed in the next thirty years.

If you are curious about how an urban-industrial area can be transformed into a thriving mixed-use neighborhood, check out the informative visitor's center at 255 Channel Street, accessed via 4th Street. *(415/437-0708; www. missionbaysf.com; open Monday to Friday 8am to 5pm; free)*

4 **SAN FRANCISCO FLOWER MART** A visit to the flower market is a fragrant, colorful treat. One of just four wholesale flower outlets left in the United States, the San Francisco Flower Mart has a history in the city longer than the stem of any rose and sweeter than its scent.

The current owners of this consortium, Rob Rossi and Mark Bechelli, are fifth- and fourth-generation California flower growers respectively. Rossi's grandfather ran several nurseries in the Excelsior District and was one of the Italian flower growers who formed the San Francisco Flower Growers Association. Meanwhile, the Japanese flower growers formed their own group, the California Flower Market. Around 1926, the two groups merged, forming the San Francisco Flower Mart.

The Flower Mart is considered the most successful flower cooperative in the United States. Although most of its operation is wholesale, the Flower Mart is open to the public, and some growers do sell retail. In addition, the cafe in the market opens early and stays open all day long. *(698 Brannan, between 5th and 6th Streets; 415/392-7944; www.sfflmart.com; open Monday to Saturday 10am to 3pm)*

5 **PACIFIC BELL PARK** The newest monument to this major-league city is its dazzling addition to major-league baseball. Pacific Bell Park (King and 3rd Streets) brings baseball back into the heart of San Francisco, here at China Basin.

From 1958 to 1961, the newly arrived San Francisco Giants played at Seals Stadium. That downtown park at 16th and Bryant was named for the minor-league San Francisco Seals, whose players included the likes of hometown boy Joe DiMaggio and his brother Dom. But city officials had promised a new stadium, and they built the boondoggle Candlestick Park **(now named** 3Com Park at Candlestick Point**) on the** coldest and windiest promontory on the bay-side. Mark Twain once said, "The coldest winter I ever spent was a summer in San Francisco." He must have been watching a game—or strolling along the shore—at Candlestick Point.

Once in Candlestick, the Giants seemed always to be ready to leave. Time and time again, they considered moving—to St. Petersburg or Toronto or anywhere that was warmer than Candlestick Point. Each time, the team was "saved" from departing by new ownership but was still stuck in baseball's windiest ballpark, where the fans were cold, a fly ball seemed uncatchable, and a pitcher was once blown off the mound. To keep attendance up for night games, the team rented blankets and awarded the Croix de Candlestick pin to each and every fan who stayed to the end of an extra-inning game.

Barry Bonds hit the first official Giants' home run in the new park on opening day, April 11, 2000. On May 1, he splashed one into China Basin (McCovey's Cove) over the right-field promenade.

Now San Francisco has a new ballpark that brings baseball back to downtown, in a stylish retro look of red-brick exterior and only-in-San-Francisco fan views of the surrounding area. Opened in April 2000, this privately financed stadium designed by HOK Sport has only 42,000 seats; each seat, by the way, is a little bit larger than an ordinary baseball-stadium seat. Appropriately enough, the park has an address of 24 Willie Mays Plaza, named after the all-time great of both the San Francisco and New York Giants. The park lies along China Basin, one of the sunniest and warmest spots in San Francisco. (Nevertheless, expect it to be cool at night.)

In Chicago, fans stand on the street to catch balls hit out of the park. San Franciscans wait in their boats in China Basin Creek for the splash of a Giants home run, and they race to scoop the ball up while it floats in the water. The Giants acceded to Don (Father Guido Sarducci) Novello's request and trained a few Portuguese Water Dogs to swim out and fetch these balls. These official retrievers work only on certain days, leaving the other days for the boat hounds.

The bridge over China Basin Creek is named for Lefty O'Doul, the great New York Giant. Along the promenade in right field overlooking the creek is a Plexiglas wall that makes it possible for those outside the stadium

The sign reading
"502" marks the
distance in feet
from home plate to
the glove in the left-
field stands, making
it Major League
Baseball's most
distant outfield
measurement sign.

to see what is going on within. The park is designed with a walking level above the promenade, which allows guests to circumnavigate the stadium. There are also four "smokestacks," reminiscent of those on a steamship, that blow steam whenever a Giant hits a home run.

Behind the center-field seats is a food court with seafood, deli, and other non-baseball foods from local restaurants. Behind the left-field seats, you can't help but notice the enormous glove and Coca-Cola bottle. The three-fingered glove, 27 feet tall, was modeled after an old-time mitt. The Coca-Cola bottle, a bit bigger than the glove, has two slides for kids and adults with good backs. Around the base of the bottle is a kids' mini-ballpark. Keep an eye on these two giant objects; they do things at appropriate moments in the game.

Getting a ticket to this popular park is difficult but is well worth the try. *(24 Willie Mays Plaza; 415/972-2000; www.sfgiants.com)*

6 SOUTH PARK AND MULTIMEDIA GULCH South Park is one of those places that always feels like a surprise, no matter how often you come upon it. The oval park between 2nd and 3rd Streets and Brannan and Bryant Streets is like an urban oasis with a distinctly European feel—it is at once peaceful and happening, surrounded by cafes, restaurants, and demure shops. In fact, South Park was designed in 1854 after London's Berkeley Square.

The idea was that the Victorian homes surrounding the grassy patch would form a European-style gated community for the city's gentry. But when the invention of the cable car in the 1870s allowed wealthy San Franciscans to develop Nob Hill, South Park lost its status and became another working-class neighborhood populated by Irish and Filipino immigrants. After the great earthquake and fire in 1906, a large segment of the city's Japanese population settled in South Park.

Today, South Park has lost its panache as a residential neighborhood but has nonetheless restored much of its luster. In addition to the retail establishments that prosper in the area, South Park is surrounded by warehouses and offices, many housing Internet start-ups and web-design firms. It has become the center of San Francisco's "Multimedia Gulch"—a neighborhood where Palm Pilots and cell phones are *de rigeur* and where dot-com entrepreneurs earn enough to retire at 29.

Jack London's birthplace is at 601 Third Street, near Brannan.

7 EMBARCADERO The waterfront boulevard known as the Embarcadero has undergone vast improvements since the freeway that once covered it came down in 1989. Opening the road was just the first step to aesthetic glory for the Embarcadero. The graceful palms were added in 1999, and the antique streetcars in 2000. New plazas and parks have gone up, and the Embarcadero—from China Basin to Fisherman's Wharf—is getting a much-deserved facelift. The San Francisco Port Commission recently approved plans to build a huge cruise ship terminal on Piers 30 and 32.

With the many changes along the Embarcadero and in the neighboring South Beach community, the city's waterfront has transformed from a place of labor disputes and industrial shipping to a glorious promenade for tourists and locals to enjoy. If you're not in the mood to skate or stroll along the water, park your car and jump out for a quick bayfront snapshot with the city's *other* famous bridge.

8 SS *JEREMIAH O'BRIEN* The National Liberty Ship *Jeremiah O'Brien* is docked here from October to May and features tours. From May to October the ship is open to the public at Pier 45 at Fisherman's Wharf. (See also the Pier 45 description in the Northern Waterfront: Fisherman's Wharf segment for more information).

9 SAN FRANCISCO–OAKLAND BAY BRIDGE There was a time when the ferries ruled the bay. East Bay commuter-rail lines brought the many commuters from Berkeley, Oakland, and points east into a port terminal in Oakland and let them ride right onto the ferries that crossed the bay to the Ferry Building.

BAY BRIDGE

Built simultaneously with the Golden Gate Bridge, the San Francisco– Oakland Bay Bridge and Tunnel opened to the public in 1936, a year before the Golden Gate Bridge. The Golden Gate Bridge was considered an architectural wonder, stretching north from the city, suspended over the mouth of the San Francisco Bay, and its beauty overshadowed the bridge-and-tunnel complex that rose to connect San Francisco to its eastern neighbors.

The Bay Bridge has two suspension bridges, a tunnel, and a cantilevered (railroad-truss type) bridge running 8.25 miles, about half of which is over water. There are two decks; originally commuter trains and trucks ran on the lower deck, but in 1958 the rail lines were replaced by buses, and the tracks were removed to create more auto and truck lanes. Today, the upper deck heads west into the city, while the lower deck heads eastward to Alameda County. More than 250,000 cars per day cross this complex. Pedestrians are not allowed.

The cantilevered section of the bridge was built where there was an underwater ridge, which provided a sturdy foundation. The tunnel was then and is still the widest ever created.

In the 1989 Loma Prieta earthquake, a section of the top roadway of the cantilevered bridge fell down onto the lower level. Although the sections, both still intact, were repaired within a month, the state's department of transportation, known as CalTrans, began studying designs for a replacement for that bridge. The design chosen—a causeway without towers— was, at last report, being revamped to include one tower. Watch for its construction, next to the cantilevered bridge east of Yerba Buena Island. Meanwhile, as with all bridges and overpasses in the state, the bridge has been retrofitted for earthquake safety while awaiting its demise. So it is safe to drive.

After it passes through the tunnel on Yerba Buena Island, there is an exit to the island itself and its artificial neighbor, Treasure Island.

10 YERBA BUENA ISLAND AND TREASURE ISLAND

Yerba Buena Island is more than just a stanchion for the sections of the San Francisco–Oakland Bay Bridge. Once known as Wood Island and then as Goat Island (goats were raised here for decades), this centerpoint in the bay formerly served as a fishing island for the Ohlone.

As the Bay Bridge tunnel was being carved out of the rock of Yerba Buena Island, the city used the debris as landfill to create Treasure Island, an area just to the north of Yerba Buena, to be the site of the Golden Gate International Exposition (GGIE) of 1939, a two-year world's fair highlighting the coming of age of San Francisco. The agreement to build this island was predicated upon turning it into San Francisco's municipal airport to replace Crissy Field near the Presidio. And, of course, it became the endpoint for the original 49-Mile Scenic Drive. (See also the introduction for more about the World's Fair and the opening of the 49-Mile Scenic Drive.)

When the fair closed, the airport was indeed established, but only Pan American Airways' China Clipper ever used it for commercial purposes, and it quickly became apparent that the field was too close to the Bay Bridge. The U.S. Navy, looking for a place to set up a training base as World War II began, made an agreement with the city to swap both islands for a large piece of bay coastline in San Mateo County so the city could establish its airport there.

Recently, the two islands were returned to civilian hands, but the city has not yet made any permanent decisions about their future use. Nonetheless, Treasure Island provides some of the most spectacular views of the San Francisco skyline and the suspension sections of the Bay Bridge. A weekend flea market also takes place there.

From Yerba Buena Island to Rincon Hill (the anchor point on the San Francisco side) is a distance of about 2 miles. This made it necessary t o build two suspension bridges to reach both ends. Because the water is deeper here—too deep to build a stanchion from the bottom up—engineers decided to build it from the top down, using a bottom-enclosed structure that was then built up until it eventually reached the floor of the bay. The cement was poured into this structure. Long tubes were placed in the mold to allow workers to then anchor the stanchion into the bedrock below.

11

FERRY BUILDING Situated where Market Street runs into the bay, the Ferry Building is a historic landmark that is finally benefiting from the flux of time. It was completed in 1898 and for almost 40 years served as the city's main public transportation hub. But with the opening of the Bay Bridge in 1936, business at the Ferry Building began a steep decline, resulting in the closing of the ferry service by 1958. Since then the Ferry Building has been largely neglected.

In a bizarre, typically San Franciscan twist of fate, the Loma Prieta earthquake of 1989 paved the way for the revitalization of the historic building. The Embarcadero Freeway that once ran from the Bay Bridge north along the Embarcadero, thereby blocking the Ferry Building from street-level view, was damaged beyond repair by the quake. When it was torn down, the Ferry Building again took its place as the crown jewel of Market Street.

The earthquake also revitalized the Ferry Building's original function. The damage it caused to the Bay Bridge halted car traffic on the bridge temporarily. For the first time in fifty years, commuters from the East Bay relied on a very small ferry system to carry them to and from San Francisco. Riding the boats was a surprising treat, and since then ferry service has remained intact between the Ferry Building and Oakland, Alameda, Larkspur, Vallejo, Sausalito, and Tiburon. Nowadays, as part of the overall project to regenerate the waterfront along the Embarcadero, plans are being made for a major renovation of the Ferry Building.

DIRECTIONS

DRIVING

To continue the Drive from the previous segment (Indiana Street at the northbound entrance to Interstate 280): Enter Interstate 280 North and follow it to its end, where it becomes a city boulevard called King Street. Follow King Street northeast; where it curves to meet the shore, it becomes the Embarcadero. Continue along the Embarcadero to the Ferry Building. (See page 182 for continued driving directions.)

PARKING

Forget about it. Parking is always tight, and when there's a ball game, it's a real challenge to find a space in this area. Metered and street parking exists but is limited. Opt instead for parking at the 5th and Mission parking garage (833 Mission, between 4th and 5th Streets) or at the Moscone Center parking garage (255 3rd Street, between Howard and Folsom Streets). These garages are not close, but they are less expensive than the parking around South Beach, which can cost as much as $2.50 per 20 minutes. Flat-rate lots ($8 to $10 per day) are more abundant around the US 101/I-80 overpass, along Stillman Street, between Bryant and Brannan near 3rd Street.

Walking from either of the public garages back to South Beach will take about 20 minutes. Consider riding the N–Judah streetcar instead. Catch it underground on Market Street, heading toward the Embarcadero. Its last stop is at 3rd and Townsend, across from Pacific Bell Park. (Make sure you take the N–Judah only; the other underground lines end at the Ferry Building.) When you're done exploring, walk or ride the streetcar back to the garage.

BUS

At 22nd Street and Pennsylvania, there is a CalTrain station. Take the train north to its terminal at 4th Street and Townsend. Or walk east on 22nd Street to 3rd Street and catch the 15–3rd Street bus, which takes you to 4th and Townsend. On the next block (3rd Street), you will find Pacific Bell Park. The E–Embarcadero and N–Judah streetcars follow King Street and the Embarcadero to the Ferry Building. (See page 182 for continued bus directions.)

WALKING

This is a long walk through uninteresting and sometimes unsafe-feeling areas. If you do walk, start at Cesar Chavez Street and Pennsylvania, turn left (north) onto Pennsylvania, and walk through the Potrero Hill neighborhood north to 7th Street. Turn left (northwest) and continue on 7th Street to King Street. Turn right (northeast) onto King Street. King Street becomes the Embarcadero. End your walk at the Ferry Building.

DOWNTOWN &
SOUTH OF MARKET

From the Financial District to Civic Center

DOWNTOWN &
SOUTH OF MARKET

Here's your chance to see the skyscraper side of San Francisco as the Drive snakes past Embarcadero Center and through the bustling Financial District. Remnants of the money-grubbing gold rush era abound down here, with small financial museums and the Pacific Stock Exchange all close by. As the Drive heads into the South of Market area ("SoMa" to locals), you'll absorb the many layers that make up this post-industrial neighborhood: Internet startups, fashionable nightclubs, and artistic installations. Stop at the contemporary urban oasis of Yerba Buena Gardens, or visit the San Francisco Museum of Modern Art. Venture just a bit off the drive and you'll find yourself on historic Market Street, with its monuments to the past and the Cable Car Turnaround at Hallidie Plaza. The Drive ends up back at City Hall, right where it started 49 miles ago.

BEST WAY TO VISIT

The streets in the downtown area can be confusing—many are one-way, and traffic is often heavy. It is best to make minimal detours from the 49-Mile Scenic Drive when exploring this area by car, or to park and walk these grand avenues of the city. Many parking spots on the streets become tow-away zones during the afternoon rush hour. We recommend that you leave your car at your hotel or at one of the public parking garages at 5th and Mission, the Moscone Center (255 3rd Street), Sutter-Stockton, or Ellis-O'Farrell, and walk or use public transportation to see the Financial District and Market and Mission Streets. Then drive the segment route to see *Defenestration* on Howard Street and find your way back to Civic Center.

THE DRIVE

EMBARCADERO CENTER Embarcadero Center, a complex of five office towers and two hotels on 10 acres, sits at the base of Market Street. With about 125 retail shops, a cinema multiplex, restaurants, and private underground parking, the towers also house many worldwide companies. The Skyview elevator brings visitors to the forty-first floor of the Embarcadero 1 building for a spectacular view of the bay. The Hyatt Regency, next to the towers and part of the overall complex, has a seventeen-story atrium and a revolving rooftop bar and restaurant. At the Hyatt, pick up a brochure describing the twenty sculptures scattered throughout the Embarcadero complex.

FINANCIAL DISTRICT OVERVIEW The city's Financial District is built upon the ghosts of rotted sailing ships and the dreams and hopes of miners and sailors. The land itself did not exist in 1849 when the gold rush began. At that time the city's shoreline was at Montgomery Street and curved down to what is now Market Street at Battery. When the city expanded into the waters of San Francisco Bay, it sank the abandoned, decaying ships that were moored in Yerba Buena Cove and used them as fill.

By the time the new coastline came into being in 1880, the land between Montgomery and the waterfront bordered by Market and Sacramento Streets had already started to become the financial center of the west. San Francisco's financiers profited by supplying the capital for those who imported, manufactured, and sold the goods needed by miners, sailors, loggers, railroad workers, farmers, and builders of homes and buildings. Rail companies such as Southern Pacific, communications companies such as Western Union and Pacific Telephone and Telegraph, utilities such as Pacific Gas and Electric, manufacturers such as Levi Strauss, and retailers such as Gumps and Shreve and Company looked to the brokers of capital for their starts and expansions. In every area of commerce, the banks and venture capitalists of the nineteenth century made money at embarrassing rates.

Financiers and businesses wanting to make San Francisco into the Rome of the Pacific—a great economic, commercial, and cultural city that would control the Pacific Rim—were stalled by the 1906 earthquake and fire, which destroyed much of the original financial district. The area bounced back again with a vengeance, however, starting with the still usable steel framing left in the rubble. Today's financial district continues to look to the Pacific Rim for its economic vitality. The streets and buildings are packed with financial moguls, stockbrokers, money managers, financial planners, accountants, and others dedicated to global commerce.

Montgomery Street is known as the Wall Street of the West, but the trading of stocks and bonds is done at the **Pacific Stock**

According to San Francisco Guide by Stephanie Gold, on the site of the pyramid there once stood a rooming house that catered to writers, including Samuel Clemens—Mark Twain. While Clemens lived at the boardinghouse, he used the public baths below the rooms. There he met a fireman one day whose name was—Tom Sawyer! And the rest is literary history.

Exchange (301 Pine Street near Sansome). Though it's usually closed to the public, a tour is available if you reserve two weeks in advance (415/393-4000). Next door is the Stock Exchange Tower, the original home of the Pacific Stock Exchange, now occupied by the City Club of San Francisco. Inside are murals painted by Diego Rivera in 1930; to see them, by appointment only, call the Mexican Museum at Fort Mason (415/202-9704). The old U.S. Customs House still stands at Washington and Battery.

Until the 1960s, the Russ Building (235 Montgomery) was the tallest building in San Francisco, at 435 feet. The tallest now is the 1971 Transamerica Pyramid (600 Montgomery Street at Columbus Avenue), an 853-foot architectural wonder. The old Transamerica Flatiron (at the intersection of Columbus, Montgomery, and Washington Streets) still has its own charms. It was built in 1909 as the headquarters for Banco Populare, and its terra-cotta design was the genius of its architects, Field and Kohlberg.

The trees in the redwood grove at the base of the Transamerica Pyramid were brought from the Santa Cruz Mountains. They make the building seem as if it were a mutant of the forest. Look in the grove for the secluded Vertigo Restaurant, and drop by on Fridays for free lunchtime concerts sponsored by the San Francisco Jazz Festival. In December, the pyramid is lighted like a Christmas tree. A free trip to the twenty-seventh floor of the building will give you magnificent views of the sights of the San Francisco Bay Area.

The Pacific Heritage Museum, housed in the Bank of Canton of California, has a permanent exhibit on the United States

Subtreasury that once stood on this spot, along with temporary and traveling exhibits on the culture, art, and history of the Pacific Rim countries. The bank's designers architecturally incorporated the 1906 four-story brick building that had replaced earlier pre-quake buildings which had at one time housed the first United States Branch Mint. *(555 Montgomery Street; 415/399-1124; open Monday to Friday 11am to 4pm; free)*

The **Wells Fargo Bank History Room** tells the story of the California gold rush. Center stage is an 1860s stagecoach, a red-and-yellow cab minus its horses. Around the corner at 464 California is Wells Fargo's world headquarters. *(420 Montgomery Street; 415/396-2619; www.wellsfargo.com/about/museum/jhtml; open Monday to Friday 9am to 5pm; free)*

Another small museum is the **Museum of the Money of the American West**, housed in the 1907 steel-and-granite **Union Bank of California** building. In the basement museum you will find a fascinating collection of privately and publicly minted coins and a history of the Comstock silver mining lode, which the bank financed. *(400 California Street; open Monday to Thursday 10am to 4pm, Friday 10am to 5pm)*

Public art is found in the **Merchant's Exchange Building and Grain Exchange Hall** (465 California Street), built in 1903. Once the offices of Julia Morgan, architect of the Hearst Castle at San Simeon, today it houses the San Francisco Chamber of Commerce and other businesses. The art comprises a group of paintings by William A. Coulter and one by Nils Hagerup. All are marine-themed oils. Inside the Old Federal Reserve Bank (400 Sansome) is *Traders of the Adriatic* by Jules Guerin, an enormous painting dating back to 1915.

2 JACKSON SQUARE HISTORIC DISTRICT The area bounded by Sansome, Pacific, Columbus, and Washington, primarily along Jackson Street, is the Jackson Square Historic District, established in

Tadich Grill (240 California; 415/391-1849), which opened in 1849, is the oldest restaurant in San Francisco. A casualty and phoenix of the 1906 quake and fire and unchanged since 1924 when it was last remodeled, it has a long hardwood bar that is crowded at lunch and dinner while patrons wait for a table.

1971. In 1906, this small area miraculously survived both the earthquake and the fire, providing one of the few glimpses we have into the post–gold rush architecture of the commercial district. Though still primarily the home of small factories and commercial tenants, Pacific Street was the dance hall/bordello area, à la the Barbary Coast; later, in the 1930s, writers and artists took over the space as businesses failed and rents dropped.

A number of transformations later, the area is now home to architectural and design-related businesses that protect the district's historical value.

3 MARKET STREET Since Irish-born city planner Jasper O'Farrell laid the plans for Market Street in 1847, this grand boulevard has been the hub of San Francisco activity, splicing downtown from the Ferry Building on the bay southwest toward Twin Peaks. When O'Farrell plotted the 120-foot-wide street on valuable land at a 36-degree angle to the streets north of it, some 400 permanent city residents were so angered that they threatened to lynch him. They didn't, and the plans for Market Street were realized. Maybe O'Farrell's grandiose plan was in fact a premonition of the growth to come. A year later gold was discovered, and the bustling metropolis of San Francisco had the massive main drag it needed.

In the 1880s cable cars and streetcars began running on Market Street. Their tracks were known as the Slot, giving rise to the nickname "South of the Slot" in reference to the area south of Market Street. A decade later, department stores started moving to Market Street, and soon after that banking institutions followed.

Market Street's "Manhattanization" began in the early 1970s. Newly built skyscrapers blocked sunlight from city streets, and Bay Area Rapid Transit, or BART, trains started carrying commuters from outlying suburbs to downtown San Francisco.

Driving on Market Street can be maddening, with the large numbers of buses, streetcars, pedestrians, and bicycles that operate on this street—combined with restrictions on left turns and lane designations. In fact, the 49-Mile Scenic Drive was moved off Market Street to Howard to help relieve traffic. By far the most pleasant way to see Market Street is to ride the F–Market antique streetcar and peacefully gaze out the window. That's probably how old O'Farrell would have wanted it anyway.

4 **MONUMENTS TO THE PAST** At the intersection of Battery and Market stands a bronze sculpture with an unusual subject. The **Mechanic's Monument** honors laborers. Built in 1895 in memory of Peter Donohue, who established California's first iron works, the sculpture shows a group of men working on a press. The piece is a product of the artistry of Douglas Tilden and the architecture of Willis Polk. Look toward your feet for bronze plaques marking the original shoreline of the cove at Yerba Buena.

On a traffic island at the intersection of Market and Kearny stands a small but proud monument, **Lotta's Fountain**. The bronze fountain was given to the city of San Francisco by Lotta Crabtree, a nineteenth-century performer. She earned her reputation—and her cash—as a bawdy San Francisco stage personality who danced for miners in the 1860s and '70s. As a sign of her affection for the city that had shown her so much love, Lotta donated the fountain to the city in 1875.

The monument played an important role during the aftermath of the 1906 earthquake, although exactly what that role was is unclear. Some say that Lotta's Fountain was a meeting place and message center for families separated during the disaster. Others remember it being a pole supporting a refugee tent. After many glorious years as one of downtown's most important landmarks, the fountain eventually fell into disrepair. In 1999 it was cleaned and restored to its original—and rightful—sheen. Water now runs in the fountain on special occasions—such as every April 18, when survivors of the 1906 quake gather at Lotta's Fountain to share memories of that fateful day and the monument that helped them through it.

Another type of monument is John's Grill at 63 Ellis, one of Dashiell Hammett's regular hangouts. First opened in 1908, the restaurant was downstairs from the Pinkerton Agency, for which Hammett worked before being disabled by tuberculosis. The grill is mentioned in *The Maltese Falcon*, and today is a celebrity stop on the restaurant scene.

5 **HALLIDIE PLAZA** One of the busiest corners in San Francisco is at Powell and Market Streets. Hundreds of people at a time line up at the Cable Car Turnaround to wait to board the Powell-Mason Cable Railway for the trip over the hills to Fisherman's Wharf. The Visitor Information Center of the San Francisco Convention and Visitor's Bureau is on the mezzanine (see the Introduction). The plaza is named for cable car pioneer Andrew Hallidie (see the Chinatown and Nob Hill segment).

SOUTH OF MARKET OVERVIEW Market Street, laid out in 1847, is a distinct dividing line in the city's layout. To pedestrians and drivers alike, the differences between the streets north and south of Market are instantly obvious. North of Market the hilly streets are narrow and the scale of development is comfortable to navigate by foot. South of Market, on the other hand, are level blocks and wide roads more suitable to car traffic. These factors have influenced the neighborhood's changing flavor throughout the years.

When it was first developed in the mid-nineteenth century, South of Market—then called South of the Slot, referring to the cable car tracks that ran along Market Street—was filled with factories, machine shops, laundries, and slums. The people who lived in the modest houses here were mostly Irish immigrants, with a few small clusters of African Americans and Asians.

When the neighborhood was rebuilt after the earthquake and fire of 1906, many of the homes and businesses were replaced with residential hotels and lodging houses where seasonal workers and merchant seamen lived—along with the city's street drunks and transients. Around this time, South of Market took on its second nickname, Skid Row.

By the mid-1950s, the building boom was beginning downtown, and along with it ideas were changing. The city's Redevelopment Agency began a huge project in the mid-1960s, resulting in today's Moscone Convention Center and Yerba Buena Gardens (described below), and displacing many of the tenants in the South of Market hotels. In the 1970s, artists and musicians began to occupy neighboring warehouses, and—as usual—gentrification loomed not far behind. By the 1980s, South of Market had emerged as San Francisco's premier nightclub district, with a new nickname, SoMa (a contraction of South of Market, in the London/New York SoHo vein).

In the 1990s, SoMa saw another transformation as the Bay Area's Internet hysteria spread. Start-ups moved into warehouses and vacant offices, and the proliferation of trendy bars, clubs, restaurants, and cafes in the SoMa area continued.

6 MISSION STREET One block east of Market is Mission Street, which starts at the Embarcadero and runs south through SoMa, the Mission District, and prolitarian residential areas to its end in San Mateo County. Its downtown component starts at the Rincon Center (Mission and Steuart Streets) and goes out to the nightclub area around 11th Street.

The **Rincon Annex of the United States Post Office,** built during the Depression, is a monument to the end of the Depression years. The art deco building is known for its murals depicting the history of California. The largest single WPA art project in the nation, the murals were painted by Anton Refregier and took about ten years to complete. Closed as a post office in 1978 and now the **Rincon Center,** a mélange of shops and offices, this member of the Register of Historic Places has carefully preserved the murals for public viewing.

Nearby, the **Jewish Museum of San Francisco** offers views of Jewish life in its continually changing exhibit space. *(121 Steuart Street; 415/591-8800; www.jewishmuseumsf.org; open Sunday to Wednesday 11am to 5pm, Thursday 11am to 8pm; admission fee, but free on Thursdays from 6 to 8pm and on the first Monday of every month)*

Just southwest of the Yerba Buena Gardens (discussed below) is the **Cartoon Art Museum.** This second-floor space exhibits the works of famous and infamous cartoonists, many from the underground comic movement. At this writing, the museum continues to look for a new street-level home. *(814 Mission Street; 415/227-8666; open Wednesday to Friday 11am to 5pm, Saturday 10am to 5pm, Sunday 1 to 5pm)*

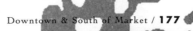

Herb Caen was a longtime San Francisco journalist who was viewed by many as the voice of the city. Of his seventy-year newspaper career, fifty-eight years were spent writing an "around town" column for the *Chronicle* and, for eight years in the 1950s, for the *Examiner*. Many people claim that before they read the front news pages, they turned to the local section to read Herb Caen. His wit—acerbic at times, punny at others—and his ongoing descriptive essays osf San Francisco added to his regular "three-dot" political and social gossip that was the heartbeat of San Francisco life.

When he died in 1997, 2,500 mourners filled Grace Cathedral for his memorial, with thousands more at a vigil, according to the *Chronicle's* coverage. "Herb's writings could make the powerful more powerful," Mayor Willie Brown said in his eulogy to Caen. "Herb's words could render the powerful harmless. Herb, your column was you, your column was your city, your column was a daily fireside chat for all of us. Farewell, dear friend."

The city named a piece of the Embarcadero in his memory, Herb Caen Way.

Across from the Yerba Buena Gardens is the new Friends of Photography **Ansel Adams Center for Photography,** a gallery focused on the naturalist photographer who lived on the central coast of California. The gallery also exhibits the works of other photographers. *(655 Mission Street; 415/495-7000; open Tuesday to Sunday 11am to 5pm, until 8pm on the first Thursday of the month)*

The original **United States Mint** (northwest corner of 5th and Mission Streets) in San Francisco was constructed in 1874. This granite structure became the main mint for the west, producing both gold and silver coins. It survived the 1906 earthquake and fire but was finally closed in 1937 when the federal government built the "new" U.S. Mint a mile away. The building is no longer open to the public because of its seismic instability.

Across the street from the old U.S. Mint, on the southwest corner of 5th and Mission, stands the **Chronicle Building** (901 Mission Street), home of Northern California's largest newspaper, the *San Francisco Chronicle*. Started in 1865 by two teenagers—Charles and Michael de Young—with a $20 loan, the *Daily Dramatic Chronicle* scooped all of its rivals when it was the first to report on Lincoln's assassination in April of that year.

In the years since then, the *Chronicle* has seen many incarnations—personalities have come and gone, and the paper's name has changed. In 1999, the *Chronicle* was bought by the Hearst Corporation, which at the time owned the *San Francisco Examiner*, the *Chronicle*'s former next-door neighbor and major rival.

The *Chronicle* has been at the 5th and Mission location since 1924. Displayed in the lobby is Pulitzer prize–winning columnist Herb Caen's typewriter—affectionately dubbed his "Loyal Royal."

7 **SAN FRANCISCO MUSEUM OF MODERN ART** One of the new tenants south of Market is the San Francisco Museum of Modern Art. Designed by the Swiss architect Mario Botta, the 1995 modern brick-and-granite building is topped by an enormous cylinder with an angled skylight as its top.

Focused on modern and contemporary art (as is its grandmother, the New York Museum of Modern Art), the museum's permanent collection includes a smorgasbord from Matisse to Rivera and Kahlo to Pollock and Rauschenberg, as well as today's established and up-and-coming names. It also has a strong photography collection, including some of the finest prints by Ansel Adams, Dorothea Lange, and others.

Visiting and temporary exhibits over the years have been as different as the Judy Chicago show in the late 1970s and the Magritte exhibition in 2000. On the ground floor, accessible without an admission fee, are the gift store and cafe. *(151 3rd Street; 415/357-4000; www.sfmoma.org; open Friday to Tuesday 11am to 6pm, Thursday 11am to 9pm; admission fee, but free the first Thursday of each month; half-price admission 6pm to 9pm on the third Thursday of each month)*

8 **YERBA BUENA GARDENS** Across the street from the Museum of Modern Art are the Yerba Buena Gardens, a remarkable landmark and a wonderful open green space. The gardens are the result of the Yerba Buena Urban Renewal Project, first proposed in the 1960s and now a green compliment to the city planners. Facing the corner of 3rd and Mission, this park is surrounded by a number of places to visit.

The Yerba Buena Center for the Arts, along the northeast side of the gardens across from the art museum, has art galleries and exhibition and performance spaces. The stage, dance, and music performances held in its 750-seat theater reflect the diverse cultural makeup of San Francisco. *(415/978-2787; www.yerbabuenaarts.org)*

The Esplanade Gardens and terraces create a relaxing place to eat lunch or while away the afternoon. To its right as you face the Center for the Arts is a band shell where live performances are held during the day. *(415/593-1718)*

A waterfall dominates the Martin Luther King Jr. Memorial. Surrounding the pool into which the water drops are granite walls engraved with famous quotes by the civil rights leader. On the face of the eastern wall is a quote from a speech Dr. King made in San Francisco in 1956: "I believe that the day will come when all God's children from bass black to treble white will be significant on the constitution's keyboard." The sound and spray of the waterfall help create a profound message of hope, peace, and tolerance that the city continues to try to embrace.

The imposing glass-and-steel building to the southwest of the gardens is the Sony Metreon, an entertainment zone with a movie-theater complex and video-game areas based on Sony-owned book and movie properties such as *Where the Wild Things Are, The Way Things Work*, and *Airtight Garage*. There are also an IMAX theater on the third floor and theme-based cafes throughout. *(415/537-3400; www.metreon.com; open daily 10am to 10pm; call for theater and exhibit hours)*

Behind the gardens is the George Moscone Convention Center. The first part of the Yerba Buena Project to open, in 1981, the convention center has hosted many of the top U.S. and international trade and industry conventions and conferences. The convention center is vast and continues to grow: New underground additions are being constructed on the center's flanks on both sides of Howard Street. *(747 Howard Street; 415/974-4000; www.moscone.com)*

Along the Howard Street side of the gardens—directly on the 49-Mile Scenic Drive—and atop the southern end of the Moscone Center is more open space: Playcircle, a children's park and playground with a great soft surface, slides, and giant balls. Roving entertainers often perform here. Across from Playcircle is Zeum, a creative, technology-centered environment for children 8 to 18. Kids can take classes in video animation or web design, or just play around with the permanent exhibits. *(415/777-2800; www.zeum.org; open Wednesday to Friday for field trips only, Saturday and Sunday 11am to 5pm)*

Between Playcircle and Zeum are a bowling alley and an ice-skating rink. Inside a nearby glass building, the Yerba Buena Carousel, originally built in 1906 for the city of San Francisco by Charles Leoff in Rhode Island, provides rides for the proverbial children of all ages. Because of the conflagration of 1906, the carousel was sold instead to Luna Park in Seattle, and it was saved in that park's fire of 1911. Brought then to San Francisco, it was a prized attraction at Playland-by-the-Sea until that park closed on Labor Day 1972. Stored for ten years, it eventually went south to Long Beach to be a tourist attraction near the *Queen Mary*. Finally, in 1998, the city of San Francisco bought it and brought it home. *(415/777-2800; open Sunday to Friday 10am to 6pm, Saturday 10am to 8pm)*

9 **DEFENESTRATION** A 3-D mural? A sculpture installation? No matter what you call it, *Defenestration* will probably make you smile. As you approach 6th Street while heading west on Howard, try to time yourself to hit a red light at that corner. On your left (the southwest corner) is an abandoned four-story building that local artist Brian Goggin has converted into a delightful work of art. Twenty-three pieces of furniture and household objects dangle from the walls and windows of the building, looking as if they've just been—vocabulary quiz—defenestrated.

10 **11TH STREET NIGHTLIFE** The place to be if you are looking for music, dancing, and other public partying is the 11th Street nightclubs. This is predominantly a late-night (after 10pm) scene. The after-hours (after 2am) clubs are sprinkled around the surrounding area. Nightclubs of every style are scattered throughout SoMa, allowing you to jump from a leather bar to a hip-hop club in just a few minutes (dress code permitting, of course). The most intense concentration of nightlife is the area around 11th and Folsom Streets. Here you'll find entertainment for every budget and taste in music—whether you're looking for punk bands or blues greats, techno fever or just a couple of beers, 11th Street can quench your thirst. More nightclubs (including many gay clubs) abound along Harrison and Folsom between 11th Street and 1st Street.

DIRECTIONS

DRIVING

To continue the Drive from the previous segment (Embarcadero at the Ferry Building):
Turn left (west) from the Embarcadero onto Washington Street. Follow it
two blocks to Battery Street. Turn left (south) onto Battery and follow
Battery to Bush Street. At Bush, bear left on Battery (all lanes can go left)
and cross Market Street, where Battery becomes 1st Street. Follow 1st
Street two blocks to Howard Street. Turn right (southwest) onto Howard
Street and follow it to 9th Street. Turn right (north) on 9th, go two blocks,
and as 9th crosses Market Street bear right onto
Larkin; turn left (west) onto Grove and right
(north) at Polk. The Drive ends at City Hall.

The often-all-ages
nightclub Slims (333
11th Street) is owned
by famous musician
Boz Scaggs.

PARKING

If you are lucky, you might get a metered parking
spot on the street. (Remember that there are tow-
away zones throughout downtown.) Most likely,
you will have to park in a garage. The city offers
garage space at 5th and Mission Streets,
Moscone Center, under Union Square, and Sutter-Stockton; all of these lots
are a 10- to 20-minute walk from the Ferry Building but are close to the F
streetcar, which you could ride to the end of Market. Private lots may be
more conveniently located, but prices can be high.

BUS

Pick up the 12–Folsom at Battery and Washington Streets and get a trans-
fer. The 12–Folsom returns to 1st Street at Market and turns west on
Howard, following the Drive to 9th and Howard Streets. Transfer to the
19–Polk at 9th and Howard. The 19 will take you back to the Civic Center.
Another option is to walk through the Financial District from the Ferry
Building, return to Market Street, and take the streetcar or any bus along
Market Street back to City Hall.

WALKING

Head north from the Ferry Building one long block to Washington Street.
Cross the Embarcadero onto Washington Street (west) and walk two blocks
to Battery Street. Turn left (south) onto Battery, which becomes 1st Street
at Market. Follow 1st two more blocks to Howard; turn right (southwest)
onto Howard and walk to 9th Street. Turn right (north) on 9th Street and
bear right when crossing Market Street. The 49-Mile Scenic Drive ends at
City Hall.

INDEX

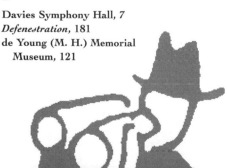